Mama Cooks
A DAY AHEAD

by Toni Reifel and Bette Woodward

Word Processed by Judy Mackel

Design and Illustration by Annette Langille Hanson

Additional copies may be obtained by addressing:

MAMA COOKS A DAY AHEAD
P. O. Box 7991
Newport Beach, California 92658

Quantity copies of Mama Cooks A Day Ahead may be obtained for
fundraising projects or by retail outlets at special discount
rates. Please write for further information.

Copyright © 1990

ISBN 0-9628049-1-6

Toni Reifel
Bette Woodward

Newport Beach, California

Bookcrafters, Inc.

Acknowledgement

Many, many thanks to everyone whose tried and true
recipes we've compiled in our cookbook, <u>Mama Cooks a Day Ahead.</u>

We appreciate your sharing these recipes with us. It is
with great pleasure that we can now share them with our readers.

"MAMA COOKS A DAY AHEAD"
INTRODUCTION

When I was a student in Boston, my roommate would invite me to go home with her on occasional weekends and holidays. Having lived in California all of my life, it was a special treat for me to visit her family in Exeter, New Hampshire.

Betty's mother was the perfect hostess. She always had interesting things planned for us to do so that I might experience the mood and local color of New England. As a result, we were never at home for any length of time as we traveled the highways and byways of New England.

However, somewhere in between our numerous activities, delicious meals would almost magically appear on the table. I'll never forget the sudden appearance of a Thanksgiving dinner with all the trimmings, steaming and hot, when Mrs. Gross had really been playing Monopoly with us all afternoon.

My curiosity finally prevailed, and I asked Mrs. Gross how she was able to accomplish this. Her answer was so simple and I've never forgotten it. She said, "I plan ahead, buy ahead, and cook at least a day ahead."

This cookbook is the result of her philosophy. I have collected make-ahead recipes for forty years, and we are hoping that with the publication of our cookbook, "Mama Cooks A Day Ahead", it will help you enjoy many extra moments with your friends and family.

Toni

"MAMA COOKS A DAY AHEAD"
INTRODUCTION

"Cooking" has always been one of my favorite pastimes. I came by it very naturally, since my grandfather was born in France and my mother cooked in a rich, nutritious and appetizing way. Cooking was always a pleasure, not a chore in our house. At a very early age, my mother encouraged me to cook and serve family meals. Those were the days when a dollar bill would buy all the makings of a delicious dinner. It delighted me to shop, cook and surprise everyone in the family with my special creations.

I married my high school sweetheart and had a family of four boys, all who definitely appreciated every meal I prepared. As my family grew up and their activities increased, I began to realize how important it was to prepare food ahead. By doing this, our mealtimes would be easier and we could keep on our busy schedules. More and more, I found that food could be prepared a day ahead and kept in the refrigerator or freezer and served, as is, or warmed in the oven or microwave, at serving time. I also realized that the flavors blended and many foods tasted even better prepared a day ahead.

Year by year, Toni and I have collected favorite recipes from our families and friends, to help make our lives simpler, and entertaining easier and more enjoyable. By using our cookbook, we hope you will enjoy our recipes too, and find "fun" by cooking in this "DAY AHEAD OF TIME WAY" !!!!!!

Bette

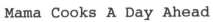
Mama Cooks A Day Ahead

TABLE OF CONTENTS

Breads
and
Special
Sandwiches

QUICK BACON AND TOMATO CRESCENTS   Makes - 8

    1 medium tomato, cut into 8 wedges
    1 (8 oz.) can refrigerator crescent dinner rolls
    8 tsp. mayonnaise or salad dressing
    8 slices cooked bacon, warm and drained
    2 Tbsp. butter or margarine, melted
    1/2 Cup cheese crackers or buttery crackers,
        crushed

Place tomato wedges on paper towel to drain. Separate crescent
dough into 8 triangles. Spread each triangle with 1 tsp.
mayonnaise. Wrap each warm bacon slice around tomato wedge: place
on wide end of each triangle. Fold corners over bacon-wrapped
tomato and roll toward opposite point of triangle. Brush all
sides of rolls with melted butter or margarine. Roll in crumbs.
Refrigerate overnight.

WHEN READY TO SERVE - Bake on ungreased cookie sheet in preheated
375° oven for 15 to 20 minutes until golden brown.

To re-heat, wrap in foil and heat at 375° for 12-15 minutes.

FROZEN BISCUITS   2 dozen

    5 Cups flour
    1 tsp. soda
    1 tsp. salt
    4 tsp. baking powder
    1 Cup Crisco
    2 pkgs. yeast
      Dissolve in 1/4 Cup water
    2 Cups buttermilk
    1 tsp. sugar

Cut shortening into dry ingredients. Add yeast and buttermilk.
Stir until dough is stiff. Roll out and cut with biscuit cutter.
Put on greased cookie sheet to freeze. Put in freezer bags and
return to freezer.

WHEN READY TO SERVE - Lightly grease cookie sheet and arrange
frozen biscuits. Put in cold oven. Set oven to 425°. NO
PREHEAT. Cook for 8-10 minutes.

CHEESE BREAD   Serves 10-12

        2 Cups cheddar cheese, grated
        1 1/2 Cups mayonnaise
        1 bunch green onions, chopped including tops
        Garlic to taste

Mix all together and spread thickly on French bread cut
lengthwise. Sprinkle with paprika and parsley flakes. Cut
serving pieces part way through. Refrigerate overnight.

WHEN READY TO SERVE - Put under broiler until slightly browned and
bubbly (about 4 minutes) or put in 350° oven for about 15 minutes.
Then finish cutting through serving pieces.

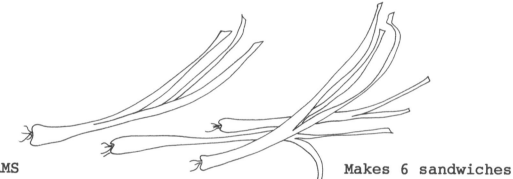

CHEESE DREAMS   Makes 6 sandwiches

        12 slices white bread
        6 slices cheddar cheese
        6 eggs
        2 Cups milk

Trim crusts from bread. Butter both sides of bread. Put cheese
(and anything else such as sliced ham, bacon, shrimp, diced green
chilies, etc.) between bread and cut in half.

Place sandwiches in baking dish. Beat eggs and milk together and
pour over bread. Be sure sandwiches are thoroughly saturated.

Refrigerate ahead if you wish to prepare day before serving but
allow to stand at least a few hours after preparing. Be sure to
place sandwiches close together.

Bake at 325° for about 45 minutes. If you wish to make larger
recipe, use larger pan and allow 1 egg and 1/3 Cup milk per
sandwich.

CHICKEN-PECAN SANDWICH FILLING   Makes 3 1/2 cups

2 Cups chicken, cooked and minced
1/2 Cup celery, finely diced
1 Cup pecans, finely chopped
1/3 Cup mayonnaise or salad dressing
1/2 tsp. seasoned salt
1/4 tsp. pepper

Mix all ingredients together, refrigerate for several hours or overnight.

Makes a delicious sandwich on wheat bread.

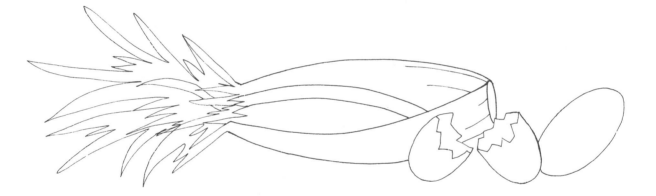

CHILI AND CHEESE CORNBREAD

1 pkg. cornbread mix
2 eggs
2 Cups cheese, grated
1 (4 oz.) can diced green chilies
1 (17 oz.) can creamed corn

Mix all the above ingredients together and pour into buttered and floured casserole. Bake at 400° for 20 to 30 minutes. This can be made a day ahead, and warmed to serve with Mexican casserole or taco salad.

CINNAMON YEAST ROLLS   Makes 4-5 dozen rolls

                    1 Cup shortening
                    1 Cup boiling water
                    1 Cup cold water
                    2 yeast cakes
                      Dissolve in 1/2 Cup warm water
                    1 tsp. sugar
                    3 eggs, beaten
                    3/4 Cups sugar
                    7-8 Cups flour
                    2 Tbsp. cinnamon
                    1/2 Cup sugar
                    1 Cup raisins

Pour boiling water over shortening. Add 1 cup cold water. Add
yeast cakes dissolved in warm water and 1 tsp. sugar. Add beaten
eggs and 3/4 cups sugar and 7-8 cups flour. Mix until not sticky.
Let rise in greased bowl until dough doubles in size. Punch down
and knead it ten times. Pinch off pieces of dough and flatten
with your hand or rolling pin on floured bread board. Cut into 1"
x 3" strips. Dip in milk, then in cinnamon and 1/2 cup sugar and
twist into tiny rolls on cookie sheet. Tuck in raisins. Bake at
350° for 10-12 minutes. Cool. Frost with thin frosting.

FROSTING: 1/2 cube butter or margarine, softened
                1/2 lb. powdered sugar
                Warm milk

Mix sugar and butter together. Add enough warm milk to make a
thin frosting.

Can be made ahead, frozen until ready to serve.

GARLIC BREAD

     1 Tbsp. garlic salt
     1/4 Cup Worcestershire sauce
     3/4 lb. sharp cheddar cheese
     1/4 Cup lemon juice
     2 tsp. paprika
     1 tsp. butter or margarine

Grate cheese (make sure it is soft). Whip everything together in blender except butter or margarine. Add margarine at the end.

Cover bowl. Refrigerate overnight or until needed. To serve, spread on sourdough bread slices and broil quickly until brown and toasty. Be careful not to burn.

We always serve this at our steak barbecues.

HAM ROLLS   Makes 12 sandwiches

     1 dozen whole wheat hot dog or hamburger buns
     1/2 lb. chopped ham (more if desired)
     4 hard cooked eggs, chopped
     1/2 Cup sliced stuffed green olives
     1 Cup cheddar cheese, grated or cubed
     1/2 Cup mayonnaise
     1/2 Cup chili sauce

Combine ham, eggs, olives and cheese with mayonnaise and chili sauce. Spread mixture inside the bun and wrap in aluminum foil to heat in oven. You can freeze these way ahead, and just pop in oven at 350° until hot and melted, when ready to eat. They are yummy, and nice to have in the freezer for unexpected guests.

LIGHT ROLLS

                    1 quart milk, scald in double boiler
                    1 Cup fresh mashed potatoes
                    1 Cup shortening
                    1 cake of yeast
                    1/2 Cup warm water
                    1 Tbsp. sugar
                    1 tsp. salt
                    1 tsp. soda
                    2 tsp. baking powder
                    4 Cups flour, sifted

Put mashed potatoes and shortening into scalded milk and let stand
until lukewarm. Dissolve cake of yeast in warm water. Let stand
for 15 minutes. Add sugar and add to milk mixture.

Mix together: Salt, soda, baking powder and flour. Add enough
flour to make a stiff dough. Knead for 15 minutes. Put in
greased bowl and let stand two hours. Refrigerate overnight and
use as needed.

When making rolls, pinch off each piece of dough to form roll.
Place on greased cookie sheet. Let rise and bake at 350° for
10-12 minutes until brown.

These can also be made ahead and frozen until time to serve.

This is an old family recipe but certainly worth the time and
energy it takes.

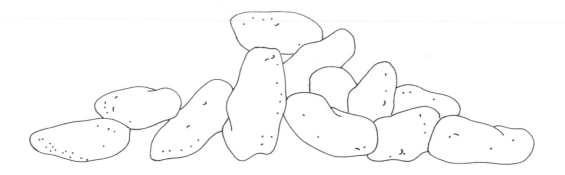

OAT BRAN MUFFINS   Makes - 1 dozen

                1 1/2 Cups Oat Bran cereal
                3/4 Cup flour
                1/4 Cup brown sugar, firmly packed
                1 Tbsp. baking powder
                1/2 tsp. salt (optional)
                3/4 Cup skim or whole milk
                1/2 Cup egg substitute or 2 eggs, beaten
                1/4 Cup honey or molasses
                2 Tbsp. vegetable oil
                1/4 Cup chopped nuts (optional)
                1/4 Cup raisins or more (optional)

Heat oven to 425°. Grease bottoms only of 12 medium size muffin
cups or line with paper baking cups. Combine dry ingredients.
Add milk, eggs, honey (or molasses) and oil. Mix just until dry
ingredients are moistened. Stir in nuts and raisins. Fill muffin
cups 3/4 full. Bake 15 to 17 minutes or until golden brown.

Store in refrigerator. They can also be frozen and served later.

WHEN READY TO SERVE - Warm in oven or microwave.

SIX WEEK MUFFINS

                1 (15 oz.) pkg. Raisin Bran cereal
                2 or 3 Cups sugar
                5 Cups flour
                5 tsp. baking soda
                2 tsp. salt
                4 eggs, beaten
                1 Cup shortening, melted
                1 quart buttermilk

Mix first five ingredients together in large bowl. Next, mix
other ingredients and combine. Store in refrigerator for at least
24 hours. Do not stir after storage. Just scoop into greased
muffin pans. Bake at 400° for 15 to 20 minutes. Batter will keep
six weeks in refrigerator.

This recipe came from a Bed and Breakfast in Newport, Rhode
Island.

PICNIC FRENCH BREAD SANDWICHES   Serves 6-8

1 1/2 lb. round loaf of sour dough French bread. Cut bread across
the center and scoop out soft bread, leaving a 1/2" to 3/4" shell.

Mix together: 1/4 Cup oil and 2 cloves crushed garlic. Brush oil
and garlic on inside shell of bread.

Fill cavity by layering the following:

> 2 tomatoes, thinly sliced
> 1 lb. luncheon meat slices
> 1/2 lb. Swiss or cheddar cheese, thinly sliced
> 1/2 lb. roast beef, thinly sliced
> 1 jar artichoke hearts, chopped
> 1 can sliced ripe olives
> 2 dill pickles, sliced
> 1 large red onion, sliced thinly

Put top on bread and press together. Cover tightly with plastic
wrap and refrigerate overnight.

WHEN READY TO SERVE - Slice like a pie and serve.

It's wonderful for a picnic.

PARTY BAKED SANDWICH LOAVES   Makes 6-8 sandwiches

1 large loaf white bread, cut in rounds made with large glass.

Filling: Mix together the following:
              2 (8 oz.) cans chicken and broth
              2/3 Cup mayonnaise
              1 (4 oz.) can chopped ripe olives
              4 hard cooked eggs, chopped

Frosting: Mix together the following:
              1 Cup butter, softened
              2 small jars Old English cheese spread
              1 raw egg

To assemble: Spread filling on bread rounds. Place one bread
              round with filling on second bread round with
              filling and top with plain bread round. Top with
              frosting.

Place on cookie sheet in refrigerator overnight. To serve, heat
in 350° oven for 15 minutes.

SANDWICH LOAF   Serves 10-12

1 large loaf un-sliced white bread: Cut off crusts and slice
length wise into four slices. Butter each large, thick slice and
spread with the following:

          Top slice: 1 (8 oz.) jar crab apple jelly

          Middle slice: 1 avocado, mashed with 2 Tbsp.
                         mayonnaise

          Bottom slice: 8 ozs. pimento cream cheese

Frost the top and sides with 1 (8 oz.) pkg. cream cheese mixed
with 1/2 Cup mayonnaise. Cover with plastic wrap and chill
overnight in refrigerator.

WHEN READY TO SERVE - Slice for each guest.

Breakfast and Brunch

SAUTEED GOLDEN DELICIOUS APPLES   Serves 6-8

    3 large Golden Delicious apples, unpeeled,
      cored and sliced thick
    3 Tbsp. butter, melted
    1 tsp. sugar

In a wide frying pan, melt butter and add apples. Cook over
moderate high heat, gently turning from time to time. When fruit
begins to soften, looks translucent and is slightly browned
sprinkle with sugar and cook for 1 minute. Place in a buttered
casserole. Cover and chill in refrigerator overnight.

WHEN READY TO SERVE - Heat uncovered in a 325° oven for 10
minutes.

This is good served with sausages.

BREAKFAST STRATA   Serves 8

    8 slices French bread, cubed
    2 Cups sharp cheese, grated
    1 1/2 lb. link sausage
    2 1/4 Cups milk
    3/4 tsp. dry mustard
    1 can cream of mushroom soup
    1/2 Cup milk
    4 eggs, beaten

In a buttered 8" x 12" baking dish place cubed bread. Sprinkle
cheese on top of bread. Brown sausage, drain and cut into pieces.
Place sausage on top of cheese and bread. Combine eggs, 2 1/4
Cups milk and dry mustard. Pour over mixture. Cover and chill in
refrigerator overnight.

WHEN READY TO SERVE - Combine soup and 1/2 Cup milk and pour over
mixture before baking for 1 1/2 hours in a 300° oven.

Delicious!

BREAKFAST SOUFFLE   Serves 8

> 8 slices bacon, cooked, drained and crumbled
> 4 Tbsp. butter
> 2 (3 oz.) pkgs. chipped beef, coarsely shredded
> 1/2 lb. fresh mushrooms, sliced
> 3/4 Cup milk
> 4 Tbsp. butter, melted
> 1/2 Cup all-purpose flour
> 1/4 tsp. pepper
> 1 quart milk
> 12 eggs, lightly beaten
> 1/4 tsp. salt

Saute mushrooms. Reserve 1/4 of the mushrooms for topping. In the same saucepan add butter and chipped beef. Mix well. Sprinkle in flour and pepper. Gradually stir in 1 1/4 Cups milk. Cook sauce until thick and smooth. Cover and set aside.

Combine eggs, salt and 2 3/4 Cups milk. Cook in butter until softly scrambled. DO NOT OVER COOK. Fold in crumbled bacon.

In a buttered 9" souffle dish layer eggs and sauce two times. Ending with sauce on top. Garnish with remaining mushrooms. Cover and refrigerate overnight.

WHEN READY TO SERVE - Bake for 20-30 minutes in a 350° oven.

This is especially nice to serve for a brunch.

BRUNCH BEEF SOUFFLE   Serves 6-8

    1 lb. ground beef
    1 1/2 tsp. salt
    1/4 tsp. black pepper
    6 eggs, well beaten
    1 1/2 Cups milk
    5 slices bread, cubed
    4 oz. Swiss cheese, grated
    1 Tbsp. pimento, diced

In a large skillet, brown meat and pour off drippings. Sprinkle
salt and pepper over beef. Mix well and allow to cool. In a
large bowl, add well beaten eggs. Beat in milk and fold in bread
cubes, cheese and pimento. Add cooled beef. Pour mixture into a
well greased 8" x 8" baking pan. Cover and refrigerate overnight.

WHEN READY TO SERVE - Bake in 325° oven for 1 hour and ten
minutes. Let stand for 5 minutes before cutting.

CHILI-CHEESE STRATA   Serves 12

    1 lb. white sandwich bread,
      crusts removed and cut into strips
    1 onion, chopped finely
    1 lb. sharp cheddar cheese, grated
    1 can chopped green chilies
    4 eggs, beaten
    3 Cups half and half
    1 tsp. Worcestershire sauce
    Salt to taste

Combine eggs, milk, Worcestershire sauce and salt together. Set
aside. In a buttered (8 1/2" x 11") casserole press bread into
dish. Top with onion, cheese and chilies. Cover with one half of
egg mixture. Repeat bread layer, onion, cheese and chilies. Add
more egg mixture. Cover and chill in refrigerator overnight.

WHEN READY TO SERVE - Bake for 45 minutes in a 350° oven.

This is our favorite Sunday morning brunch dish!

CHILI EGG PUFF   Serves 10

    10 eggs, beaten
    1/2 Cup flour
    1 tsp. baking powder
    1/2 tsp. salt
    1 pint small curd cottage cheese
    1 lb. jack cheese, grated
    1/2 Cup butter, melted
    2 (4 oz.) cans diced green chilies, seeded

Beat eggs until light. Add flour, baking powder, salt, cottage
cheese, jack cheese and butter. Stir in chilies. Pour mixture
into a buttered 13" x 9" baking dish. Cover and refrigerate
overnight.

WHEN READY TO SERVE - Bake in a 350° oven for 35 minutes or until
brown and center is firm.

CHILI RELLENO CASSEROLE   Serves 6-8

    1 lb. jack cheese, grated
    1 lb. cheddar cheese, grated
    1 (27 oz.) can green chilies, seeded
    1 Cup evaporated milk, very cold
    2 eggs, beaten
    1/2 Cup flour
    Salt to taste
    1 can tomato sauce

In a buttered 13" x 9" casserole layer chilies and cheese. Beat
together very cold milk and eggs. Add and beat in flour and salt.
Pour mixture over chilies and cheese. Cover and refrigerate
overnight.

WHEN READY TO SERVE - Bake for 25 minutes in a 350° oven. Remove
from oven and pour over 1 can of tomato sauce and return to oven
for 7 minutes. Let stand for 5 minutes before cutting and
serving.

A great Brunch dish!

CREPES   Serves 8-10

3 eggs, beaten
1 Tbsp. butter or margarine, melted
1 Cup all-purpose flour, sifted
1/4 Cup sugar
1/4 tsp. salt
1 1/2 Cups milk

Beat eggs and butter together until well blended. Alternate
adding dry ingredients with milk when adding to egg mixture.
Cover and allow to stand at room temperature for 2 hours.

Preheat crepe pan over medium heat. Lightly brush pan with
butter. Pour 2-3 Tbsp. of batter into center of pan and
immediately rotate pan to cover entire bottom surface with a very
thin layer of batter. Cook over heat until top of crepe is dry
and the underside is delicately browned. Turn crepe with spatula
and cook until lightly browned. Stack crepes on top of each other
with wax paper separating each one until ready to use. Crepes can
be made ahead and held in refrigerator covered in foil until ready
to fill.

WHEN READY TO SERVE - Bring crepes to room temperature. Fill
crepe with fresh fruit for dessert or with creamed chicken or crab
when served as a main dish at a luncheon or Brunch.

COUNTRY GRITS AND SAUSAGE   Serves 8

        1/2 Cup quick grits, uncooked
        2 cups water
        1/2 tsp. salt
        4 Cups cheddar cheese, grated
        4 eggs, beaten
        1 Cup milk
        1/2 tsp. Thyme
        1/8 tsp. garlic salt
        2 lbs. mild pork sausage, cooked, drained and crumbled
        1 fresh tomato, sliced (garnish)
        Parsley sprigs (garnish)

Bring 2 cups water and 1/2 tsp. salt to a boil. Add grits, stirring constantly. Bring to a boil and reduce heat. Cook for 4 minutes, stirring constantly. Drain.

Combine grits with cheese in a large mixing bowl. Stir until cheese is melted. Combine eggs, milk, thyme and garlic salt. Mix well. Add small amounts of grits to egg mixture until all are well mixed. Add sausage and mix well. Fold into a 12" x 8" buttered baking dish. Cover and refrigerate overnight.

WHEN READY TO SERVE - Let stand at room temperature for 20 minutes. Bake at 350° uncovered for 45-50 minutes, or until set. Garnish with tomato slices and parsley sprigs.

This is good served with fresh fruit at a brunch.

EGG CASSEROLE   Serves 6

    1 lb. sausage, browned, crumbled and drained
    2 Cups milk, warmed
    2 (5 oz.) jars of prepared soft cheese
    6 slices bread, without crusts
    6 eggs, beaten
    1 tomato, chopped
    1 onion, chopped
    1/4 lb. fresh mushrooms, chopped
    1 tsp. dry mustard
    Salt and pepper to taste

Brown sausage with onion and mushrooms. Drain and remove drippings. Add warm milk and cheese and stir until melted. Add beaten eggs and tomato to sausage mixture and mix well. Break up bread slices and add to mixture. Pour into a buttered 13" x 9" casserole. Cover and refrigerate overnight.

WHEN READY TO SERVE - Bake casserole covered with foil in a 350° oven for 1 hour uncovered for last 10 minutes to brown.

GRANOLA   Serves 20-24
Excellent cereal

    6 Cups old fashioned oats
    2 Cups wheat germ
    1-2 cups assorted unsalted nuts, chopped
    1 1/2 Cups brown sugar
    3/4 Cup salad oil
    1/2 Cup honey
    raisins
    dates, chopped

Heat together oil and honey. Add remaining ingredients and mix
well. On cookie sheets, spread out mixture and bake for 5
minutes in a 350° oven. With a spatula turn mixture and bake for
another 5 minutes. Allow to drain on paper towels. Add raisins
and cut up dates to mixture and store in airtight containers.
Flavor is enhanced after 24 hours of storage.

This mixture keeps for a long time.

HAM QUICHE   Serves 6-8

    1/2 lb. fresh mushrooms, sliced
    2 Tbsp. butter
    1 Cup sour cream
    1 Cup small curd cottage cheese
    1/4 Cup flour
    1 tsp. onion powder
    Dash of Tabasco
    2 Cups jack cheese, grated
    1/2 Cup ham, diced
    4 eggs, slightly beaten

Saute mushrooms in butter and cook until lightly browned. Drain
and set aside. Combine remaining ingredients. Add mushrooms and
pour into a 10" buttered quiche pan. Cover and store in
refrigerator overnight.

WHEN READY TO SERVE - Bake for 45-50 minutes in a 350° oven or
until browned on top.

MUSHROOM AND SPINACH QUICHE   Serves 8

Crust: 1 Cup pastry flour
                1 cube butter
                1/2 Cup cream cheese
                Dash of salt

Cut butter and cheese into flour and salt. Blend well and press
dough an oiled plate.

Mixture: 3 Cups jack, cheddar or Swiss cheese, grated
                1/4 Cup onions, diced
                1/4 Cup parsley, chopped
                1 1/2 Cup fresh mushrooms, cooked and drained
                1/2 bunch fresh spinach leaves

Saute mushrooms in 2 Tbsp. sherry and 2 Tbsp. butter. Drain and
set aside. Line the quiche crust with 2 cups cheese. Sprinkle
cheese with onions and parsley. Add a layer of mushrooms and top
with spinach leaves.

Filling: 1/2 cube butter, melted
                1/4 Cup flour
                4 eggs, beaten

Melt butter and flour together, stirring constantly and cook until
it smells nutty. Remove from heat and add eggs. Mix well. Pour
over quiche. Cover and refrigerate overnight.

WHEN READY TO SERVE - Bake for 40 minutes in a 325° oven.
Sprinkle remaining cup of cheese on top and return to oven and
bake until melted.

De..eelicious!!!

HERBED SPINACH QUICHE   Serves 4-6

    2 Cups ham, diced
    2 (10 oz.) pkgs. frozen spinach, cooked and drained
    2 Cups rice, cooked
    2 Cups cheddar cheese, grated
    4 eggs, slightly beaten
    4 Tbsp. butter or margarine, soften
    2/3 Cups milk
    4 Tbsp. onion, chopped
    1 tsp. Worcestershire sauce
    1 tsp. salt
    1/2 tsp. Rosemary, crushed

Combine all ingredients and pour into a buttered 9" x 13" pan.
Cover and refrigerate overnight.

WHEN READY TO SERVE - Let stand at room temperature for 20 minutes
before baking for 40-45 minutes in a 350° oven or until knife
inserted in center comes out clean. Sprinkle a little extra
cheese on top and return to oven for 5 minutes.

Excellent for appetizer. Cut into small squares to serve 12.
The recipe can be halved and baked in a pie shell. Serves 4-6

This is a very popular brunch dish!

KRASNAPOLSKY

    2 (10 oz.) pkgs. frozen chopped spinach, thawed and dry
    6 eggs, beaten
    2 pint cartons creamed cottage cheese
    1/2 lb. sharp cheddar cheese, grated
    1/4 lb. butter, softened
    4-6 Tbsp. flour

Mix ingredients together and put in a lightly buttered casserole.
Cover and refrigerate overnight.

WHEN READY TO SERVE - Bake covered in a 350° oven for 1 hour.

A great brunch dish.

SPINACH QUICHE IN CHEESE-RICE CRUST   Serves 6

Crust: 1 egg white, lightly beaten
                1 tsp. soy sauce
                1/4 Cup Parmesan cheese, grated
                1/4 tsp. pepper
                1 1/2 Cups rice, cooked

Mix together egg white with soy sauce. Add cheese and pepper.
Stir in cooked rice. Blend well. Press into a buttered 9" quiche
pan and bake for 25-30 minutes in a 375° oven. Cool and set
aside.

Filling: 2 (10 oz.) pkgs. frozen chopped spinach,
                  thawed and dry
                1/4 milk
                1 Tbsp. arrowroot
                Salt, pepper and nutmeg to taste
                3 egg yolks
                3 egg whites
                4 oz. jack cheese, cut into strips

In food processor chop spinach until smooth. Drain and reserve
liquid. In a saucepan heat milk and add arrowroot. Stir until
thickened. Add drained spinach liquid. Add seasonings. Add egg
yolks. Mix well and allow to cool. Beat egg whites until stiff
and fold into mixture. Pour into pie crust. Cover and
refrigerate overnight.

WHEN READY TO SERVE - Make a lattice work top with cheese on top
of quiche and bake for 20 minutes in a 400° oven.

Delicious!

QUICHE LORRAINE CASSEROLE   Serves 8-10

        1/2 Cup butter
        10 eggs, slightly beaten
        1 tsp. baking powder
        2 Tbsp. flour
        1/2 tsp. salt
        1 (7 oz.) can chopped chilies
        1 (16 oz.) carton cottage cheese
        1 lb. jack cheese, grated

Butter a 13" x 9" casserole. In a large bowl, mix together eggs,
flour, baking powder. Add butter, chilies, cottage cheese and
jack cheese. Mix until smooth and well blended. Turn mixture
into casserole. Cover and refrigerate overnight.

WHEN READY TO SERVE - Bake for 15 minutes at 400°. Reduce heat
and bake for 35-40 minutes in 350° oven.

SOUTH OF THE BORDER QUICHE   Serves 6-8

    1 prepared pie crust
      Add 1 tsp. chili powder when preparing pie crust
    3/4 Cup cheddar cheese, grated
    1/2 Cup jack cheese, grated
    3 eggs, beaten
    1 tsp. salt
    Salt and pepper to taste
    1 1/2 Cups half and half
    1 (4 oz.) can diced olives
    2 Tbsp. green onions, chopped

Press cheeses into pie crust. Mix together remaining ingredients
and pour into crust. Cover and refrigerate overnight.

WHEN READY TO SERVE - Bake for 40-45 minutes in 350° oven or until
brown on top.

Great for a Brunch.

SOURDOUGH PANCAKES   Makes 24

    2 Cups flour
    2 Cup sour dough starter
    1 Cup milk
    2 eggs, beaten
    1/4 Cup sugar
    1/4 Cup oil
    1 Tbsp. baking powder
    1 Tbsp. salt
    1 Tbsp. soda

Beat until smooth flour, starter and milk. Cover loosely and let
stand in a warm place for 24 hours. Add remaining ingredients and
stir until smooth.

WHEN READY TO SERVE - Bake on a hot buttered griddle using 1 Tbsp.
butter for each pancake.

We had these in Alaska and they are really good.

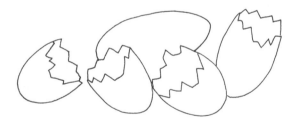

SWEDISH PANCAKES   Makes 6-8

    1/2 cup flour
    1 Tbsp. sugar
    Pinch of salt
    2 eggs, beaten
    1 1/2 Cups milk

Sift together flour, sugar and salt. Set aside. Beat eggs with
milk. Add dry ingredients and beat until smooth. Cover and chill
batter overnight.

WHEN READY TO SERVE - Beat batter again until smooth. Bake on a
hot, lightly greased griddle. Serve with preserves.

PRALINE BRUNCH TOAST   Serves 4-6

        8 eggs, beaten
        1 1/2 Cups milk
        1/2 Cup + 1 Tbsp. brown sugar
        2 tsp. vanilla
        8 slices French bread, 3/4" thick
        1/4 Cup butter
        1/4 Cup maple syrup
        1/2 Cup pecans, chopped

Thoroughly blend together, eggs, milk, 1 Tbsp. brown sugar and
vanilla. Pour half of egg mixture into a 13" x 9" baking dish.
Place bread slices into baking dish with egg mixture. Pour
remaining egg mixture over top. Cover and refrigerate overnight.

WHEN READY TO SERVE - Melt butter in another 13" x 9" baking dish
in a 350° oven. Stir into baking dish brown sugar and syrup.
Sprinkle with pecans. Carefully place soaked bread slices into
baking dish and pour any remaining mixture over top. Bake for 30-
35 minutes in a 350° oven or until puffed and lightly browned.
Invert to serve.

This is like a party French toast.

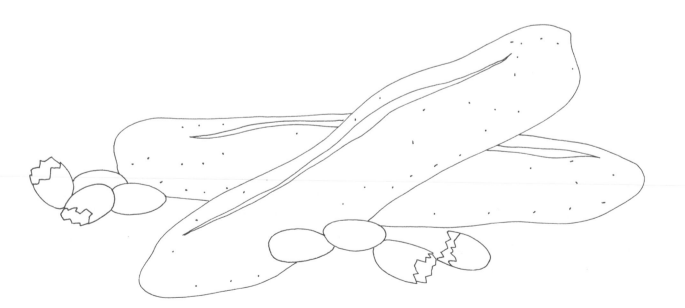

Desserts

ANGEL PIE

Serves 6-8

    4 egg whites, stiffly beaten
    1/2 tsp. cream of tartar
    1 Cup sugar

Add cream of tartar to stiffly beaten egg whites and gradually add
sugar. Spread evenly over a well buttered and floured pie tin.
Keep away from the edges. Bake for 20 minutes at 275°, and then
40 minutes in a 300° oven.

Filling: 4 egg yolks
                  1/2 Cup sugar
                  1 Tbsp. lemon juice
                  2 Tbsp. pineapple juice
                  Rind of one lemon

Cook together the above ingredients in a double boiler. Cook for
8 minutes or until the mixture thickens and coats a spoon. Set
aside.

                  1 Cup whipping cream
                  1 tsp. sugar

Whip together whipping cream and sugar. Spread one half of the
mixture into pie shell. Add one quarter of the remaining whipped
cream mixture to egg and lemon filling mixture and pour into pie
shell. Top with remaining whipped cream. Cover and refrigerate
overnight.

APPLE BROWN BETTY

Serves 8

    2 lb. tart green apples, peeled and sliced
    1 Tbsp. lemon juice
    1/2 Cup sugar
    1 tsp. cinnamon
    1/4 tsp. nutmeg
    3/4 Cups graham cracker crumbs
    1/2 Cup oats
    3/4 Cup brown sugar
    1/2 Cup butter, cold and cut into 8 pieces
    1/2 Cup walnuts or pecans, chopped
    1/2 Cup sour cream (topping)
    2 Tbsp. powdered sugar (topping)
    1/2 tsp. vanilla (topping)

Sprinkle lemon juice, sugar and spices over apples and toss. Set aside. Combine crumbs, oats, brown sugar and cold butter . Mix until crumbly. Stir in nuts. Sprinkle one half of the mixture over bottom of a 9" or 10" buttered pie plate. Layer apples over crumbs and top with remaining crumbs. Bake in 375° oven for 30 minutes. Cover and refrigerate overnight.

WHEN READY TO SERVE - Mix together topping ingredients and serve on warmed brown betty.

ALMOND CHEESE CAKE
                                                    Serves 12

Crust: 1 3/4 Cups graham cracker crumbs
                       Reserve 1/2 Cup for topping
                    1/2 tsp. ground cinnamon
                    1/2 Cup butter, melted

Blend thoroughly and press into a greased spring-form pan with
mixture covering bottom and sides of pan.

Filling: 2 (8 oz.) pkgs. cream cheese
                    1 Cup sugar
                    3 eggs, well beaten
                    3 Cups sour cream
                    1 1/2 tsp. vanilla
                    3/4 tsp. almond extract
                    Dash of salt

Cream together cream cheese and sugar. Add beaten eggs and beat
well. Add salt and seasonings. Beat well. Add sour cream and
blend. DO NOT BEAT. Pour over crust and sprinkle remaining
crumbs on top. Bake for 40 minutes in a 375° oven or until set.
Filling will look very soft. Cover and chill overnight in the
refrigerator.

FRESH APPLE NUT CAKE

Serves 10-12

    3 eggs
    2 Cups sugar
    1 Cup salad oil
    1 tsp. vanilla
    1 1/4 tsp. soda + 4 tsp. water
    1/2 tsp. nutmeg
    1 tsp. cinnamon
    1 tsp. salt
    1/2 tsp. cloves
    3 Cups flour
    3 Cups fresh apples, diced
    1 Cup pecans or walnuts, chopped

Mix first 10 ingredients together in order of recipe. Add apples
and nuts. Beat by hand until thoroughly mixed. Butter a bundt
pan or spring pan generously and fold in mixture. Bake for 1 hour
at 375°. Remove from oven and place in paper bag until it cools.
Delicious when kept in the bag overnight.

Topping: Frost before serving with powdered sugar, milk and
                butter frosting. Make it thick.

APPLE PUDDING

Serves 8

    1 Cup sugar
    1 egg
    1/4 Cup margarine
    2 apples, peeled and cut into pieces
    1 Cup flour
    1/2 tsp. soda
    1 tsp. cinnamon
    Nuts (optional)
    Whipped topping

Mix all ingredients together and fold into a well buttered 8"
pyrex cake pan. Bake for 30 minutes in a 350° oven. Cover and
chill overnight in the refrigerator.

WHEN READY TO SERVE - Top with whipped topping at serving time and
sprinkle with cinnamon.

NO-BAKE BANANA SPLIT CAKE

Serves 12

Crust: 1 1/2 cubes butter or margarine, cold
                  3 Cups graham cracker crumbs

Cut cold butter into graham cracker crumbs. Press mixture into a
9" x 13" pan. Set aside.

Filling: 2 cubes butter or margarine
                  2 eggs
                  2 Cups powdered sugar

Beat together butter, eggs and powdered sugar until smooth, about
20 minutes. Smooth over pie crust.

                  5 bananas, sliced into thirds lengthwise
                  1 large can crushed pineapple, drain
                    and reserve liquid
                  1 (16 oz.) carton whipped topping
                  Nuts, chopped
                  Cherries, chopped
                  Chocolate syrup

Dip sliced bananas into reserved pineapple juice to keep from
darkening. Spread crushed pineapple into pie crust. Spread
whipped topping into pie crust. Arrange sliced bananas and
sprinkle with nuts and cherries. Drizzle chocolate syrup over
top. Cover and chill overnight.

Wow! This is yummy.

APRICOT CHEESE DELIGHT

Serves 12

        1 can apricots, drained and cut finely (reserve liquid)
        1 can crushed pineapple, drained (reserve liquid)
        1 (6 oz.) pkg. orange Jell-O
          Dissolve in 1 cup boiling water
        2 Cups water
        1 Cup of combined apricot and pineapple juice
        3/4 Cup miniature marshmallows

Dissolve Jell-O in boiling water. Cool and excluding
marshmallows, add remaining ingredients. Fold in marshmallows and
pour into a water rinsed 11" x 7" x 2" baking dish. Cover and
chill overnight in the refrigerator.

Topping: 1/2 Cup sugar
                2 Tbsp. flour
                1 egg, slightly beaten
                1 Cup combined apricot and pineapple juice
                2 Tbsp. butter
                1 Cup heavy cream, whipped
                3/4 Cup cheese, grated

Combine sugar and flour and blend in beaten egg. Gradually stir
in juices and while stirring over low heat cook until thick.
Remove from heat and stir in butter. Cool. Fold in whipped cream
and spread over Jell-O layer. Sprinkle with grated cheese.

BAILEY'S IRISH CREAM

Serves 6

        1 1/2 Cups half and half
        1 Cup heavy cream
        3 eggs
        3/4 Cups sugar
        1 tsp. vanilla
        1/2 Cup Bailey's Irish Cream liqueur
        4 oz. semi-sweet chocolate chips, melted

In a saucepan, whisk together half and half, cream, eggs and
sugar. Heat, whisking constantly until mixture is a custard.
About 7-8 minutes. Remove from heat and whisk until cool. Add
vanilla and liqueur. Place mixture into an ice cream freezer tray
for 10 minutes. Remove from freezer and drizzle on chocolate.
Return to freezer overnight to bring out the flavor.

BROWNIE PIE

Serves 6-8

    3 egg whites
    Dash of salt
    3/4 Cup sugar
    3/4 Cup chocolate wafers, rolled fine
    1/2 Cup walnuts, chopped
    1/2 pint whipping cream, whipped and sweetened
    1 tsp. vanilla

Beat egg whites and salt until soft peaks form. Add sugar slowly
and beat until stiff peaks form. Fold in chocolate wafer crumbs,
nuts and vanilla. Spread evenly in a buttered 9" pie pan. Bake
for 35 minutes in a 325° oven. Cool thoroughly and spread with
whipped cream. Cover and chill overnight in the refrigerator.

BUTTERFLY DESSERT

Serves 12

    1 large day old Angel Food cake
    1 pkg. orange Jell-O
    2 Cups orange juice
    1/2 pint whipping cream
    1 large can crushed pineapple, drained
    1 can Mandarin oranges, drained

Dissolve Jell-O in 1 cup of boiling water or orange juice. Add 1
cup cold orange juice to dissolved Jell-O. Refrigerate until
goopy. Tear apart cake. Set aside. Add pineapple to Jell-O
mixture. Beat the whipping cream until stiff. Add 1/2 of whipped
cream to jell-O mixture. Set aside.

In the bottom of a 9" x 12" pan make a layer of cake. Top with
one half of the orange mixture. Repeat until reaching the top.
Cover and chill overnight in the refrigerator.

WHEN READY TO SERVE - Top with remaining whipped cream and
Mandarin orange slices.

This is a very special dessert. Especially nice for a shower and
ladies luncheon.

CHARLOTTE AUX POMMES
apple dessert

Serves 12

        7 lb. pippin apples, peeled and sliced
        1 Cup butter, melted
        1 Tbsp. vanilla
        3/4 Cups sugar
        4 Tbsp. apricot jam, sieved
        A pinch of cinnamon
        12 slices of white bread, crusts removed
        3 Tbsp. rum
        1/2 pint whipping cream, whipped

In a skillet place apples and add 1 tsp. water, sugar and
cinnamon. Bring to a boil. Reduce heat to a simmer and cover for
15 minutes. Checking to see apples are not sticking. Add
vanilla, rum and jam. Stir and cook for 10 minutes longer or
until apples resemble a thick marmalade. Dip each bread slice
into melted butter and arrange on the bottom and sides of a
spring form pan. Pour apple marmalade into mold and cover with
bread slices. Cover and refrigerate overnight.

THE NEXT DAY - Bake for 35 minutes in a 400° oven. Run a knife
between mold and bread slices to remove from pan.

WHEN READY TO SERVE - Top with a dollop of sweetened whipped
cream. May be served hot or cold.

Delicious!

CHESS TARTS
                                                         Serves 8

Crust: 1 cube butter, softened
                1 (3 oz.) pkg. cream cheese
                1 Cup flour

Mix butter and cream cheese together with a fork. Add flour and
mix well, until it forms a ball. Make a walnut size ball and
press into shape in a tart pan. Keep cool and set aside.

Filling: 2 Cups sugar
                1 Cup butter
                4 egg yolks
                3 Tbsp. vinegar
                1/2 tsp. vanilla
                1/2 tsp. cinnamon
                1/2 tsp. allspice
                1/2 tsp. cloves
                1 Cup nuts
                1 Cup raisins
                4 egg whites, stiffly beaten

Cream together sugar and butter. Add egg yolks beaten first with
vinegar. Add seasonings and mix well. Add nuts and raisins.
Fold in egg whites and place in tart pans.

Bake in a slow oven for about 1 hour. When cooled, cover and
place in refrigerator overnight.

WHEN READY TO SERVE - Serve with a dollop of whipped cream.

CHEESE CAKE

Serves 8

        2 (8 oz.) pkgs. cream cheese, softened
        3 eggs
        2/3 Cups sugar
        1/4 tsp. almond or lemon extract
        2 Cups sour cream
        3 Tbsp. sugar
        1 tsp. vanilla
        Fresh fruit (garnish)

Beat cheese until light and creamy. Add eggs, one at a time and beat until smooth. Add sugar and extract. Beat until smooth, (about 5 minutes). In a well greased 9" or 10" pyrex pan fold in mixture and bake for 50 minutes in a 325° oven. Cool.

For topping, beat together sour cream and 3 Tbsp. sugar and vanilla. Spoon over cake. Cool at room temperature. Crust forms as the cake cools. Cover and refrigerate overnight.

WHEN READY TO SERVE - Garnish with fresh fruit.

Always a favorite.

CHOCOLATE ANGEL CAKE

Serves 8-10

        1 large Angel Food cake
        1 large pkg. chocolate chips
        2 Tbsp. sugar
        3 egg yolks, beaten
        3 egg whites, beaten
        1 pint whipping cream, stiffly beaten
        1/2 tsp. vanilla

Break up the cake. Place half of the cake into a greased 8" x 12" pan. Set aside. Melt chocolate chips with sugar in double boiler. Add egg yolks and mix well. Remove from stove and cool for 5 minutes. Add egg whites, whipped cream and lastly, vanilla. Pour half of the mixture over the broken up cake. Add remaining cake pieces and top with chocolate mixture. Cover and refrigerate overnight.

CHOCOLATE CHIP MERINGUES

Serves 4-6

    2 egg whites
    1/2 Cup sugar
    1 Cup chocolate chips
    1 Cup walnuts, chopped
    1/2 tsp. vanilla
    Pinch of salt

Preheat oven to 350°. Add vanilla and salt to egg whites. Beat until frothy. Gradually add sugar, beating until stiff and forming peaks. Fold in chocolate chips and nuts. Drop by the teaspoon on a greased cookie sheet. Place in oven. CLOSE DOOR AND TURN OFF HEAT. Leave meringues in oven overnight and do not open the door until morning.

WHEN READY TO SERVE - Serve with ice cream and chocolate sauce.

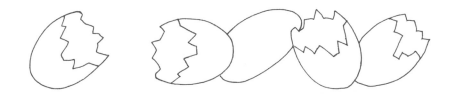

CHOCOLATE CHUNK ICE CREAM PIE

Serves 6

    1 cup milk, cold
    1/2 pint chocolate ice cream, softened
    1 (3 oz.) pkg. milk chocolate pudding mix
    4 squares semi-sweet chocolate, cut into chunks
    1 prepared graham cracker pie crust
    8 oz. whipped topping

Blend together milk and ice cream. Add pudding mix. Beat at lowest speed on mixer until well blended. About 1 minute. Fold in chocolate chunks. Pour into crust. Cover and place in freezer overnight.

WHEN READY TO SERVE - Place pie in refrigerator 20 minutes before serving. Garnish with whipped topping and shaved chocolate, if desired. Store left over pie back in freezer.

CHOCOLATE ECLAIR CAKE

        36 graham crackers, whole
        1 small pkg. vanilla pudding mix
        18 oz. container of whipped topping
        3 Cups milk
        1 can chocolate frosting or homemade frosting

Line a buttered 13" x 9" pan with whole graham crackers. Mix
pudding mix and milk together. Cook mix until thickened. Remove
from heat and cool. Add whipped topping. Pour half of the
mixture over the graham crackers and top mixture with another
layer of crackers on top. Swirl the frosting as you would on a
cake. Cover and refrigerate overnight.

CHOCOLATE MARVEL PIE

                                                    Serves 6-8

        1 pkg. semi-sweet chocolate bits
        3 Tbsp. milk
        2 Tbsp. sugar
        4 egg yolks
        4 egg whites
        1 tsp. vanilla
        1 prepared pie crust
        1/2 pint whipping cream, whipped

Cook pie crust. Cool and set aside. In a double boiler melt
chocolate bits, milk and sugar. Cool. Add egg yolks one at a
time. Beat well after each yolk is added. Beat egg whites until
stiff and fold into chocolate mixture. Fold into pie crust.
Cover and chill overnight.

WHEN READY TO SERVE - Garnish with whipped cream.

CHOCOLATE TORTE

Serves 6

    3 egg whites
    1/2 tsp. vanilla
    Dash of salt
    3/4 Cup sugar
    3/4 Cup chocolate wafers, crushed
    1/2 Cup walnuts, chopped
    1 Cup whipped cream, sweetened (topping)
    1 square unsweetened chocolate, grated (topping)

Beat egg whites, vanilla and salt together until foamy.
Gradually add sugar. Beat until stiff, not dry. Fold in crushed
chocolate wafers. Spread lightly in a buttered 9" pie plate.
Bake for 35 minutes in a 325° oven. Cool. Top with whipped
cream. Cover and chill overnight in the refrigerator.

WHEN READY TO SERVE - Top with whipped cream and grated chocolate.

This recipe is so good, we usually double the recipe to serve a
larger group.

CRAZY PIE

Serves 6-8

    3 egg whites, beaten into soft peaks
    1 Cup sugar
    15 Ritz crackers, crumbled
    3/4 Cup pecans, chopped
    1/2 tsp. almond extract
    Pinch of baking powder
    1/2 pint whipping cream, whipped

Slowly add sugar to beaten egg whites. Slowly add remaining
ingredients. Fold mixture into a greased pie tin. Bake for 25
minutes in a 325° oven. Cool. Cover and chill overnight in the
refrigerator.

WHEN READY TO SERVE - Dollop each piece with whipped cream.

DEATH BY CHOCOLATE

Serves 8

        1 prepared chocolate pie crust
        1 pint rocky road ice cream, softened
        1 pint chocolate fudge ice cream, softened
        2 Twix candy bars, cut up
        Chocolate sauce

Mix together ice cream and candy bars. Place into a pie shell.
Freeze overnight.

WHEN READY TO SERVE - Heat chocolate sauce and pour over ice cream
pie.

This is for chocolate lovers only!

E-Z CAKE

Serves 12

        2 Cups flour
        2 Cups sugar
        2 eggs
        2 tsp. baking soda
        1 large can crushed pineapple, undrained
        1 Cup walnuts, coarsely cut

By hand, mix all the ingredients together. Pour into a greased
9" x 13" pan. Bake in 40 minutes in a 350° oven. Cool slightly.

Frosting:

                1 (8 oz.) pkg. cream cheese
                1 cube butter or margarine
                2 Cups confectioners sugar
                1 tsp. vanilla

Combine and mix the frosting ingredients and beat until smooth.
Pour over cake while still warm. Cover and chill in refrigerator
overnight.

Don't cut pieces too large, very rich!

FRENCH ORANGE CAKE

Serves 18-20

        1 Cup shortening
        2 Cups sugar
        2 eggs
        4 Cups cake flour, sifted
        2 tsp. baking powder
        1 tsp. salt
        2 tsp. vinegar
        2 Cups milk
        2 tsp. soda
        2 tsp. cold water
        1 Cup dates, chopped
        1 Cup walnuts, chopped

TOPPING: 1 Cup orange juice
                1 Cup sugar

Cream shortening and sugar. Add eggs, one at a time, beating each
egg in thoroughly. Sift together, flour, baking powder and salt.
Add vinegar to milk. Add sifted dry ingredients to egg mixture,
alternating with milk. Add soda to water and pour over dates.
Add dates and nuts to batter. Batter will be very thin. Pour
into a greased 10" angel food pan and bake for 1 hour in a 350°
oven.

While cake is hot, pour over a mixture of 1 cup of orange juice
and 1 cup of sugar. Cover and refrigerate overnight.

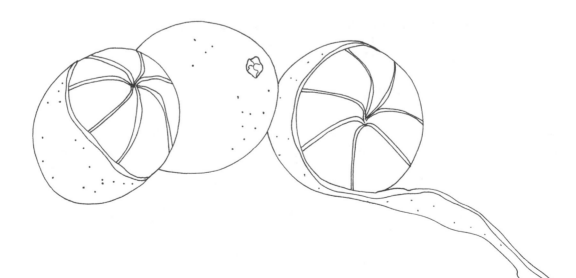

FRANGO MINT DESSERT

Serves 12-14

    1 Cup butter
    2 Cups powdered sugar, sifted
    4 squares unsweetened chocolate, melted
    3/4 tsp. peppermint extract
    4 eggs
    2 tsp. vanilla
    1 Cup vanilla wafer crumbs

Cream together butter and sugar. Add melted chocolate and blend
well. Mix in eggs and flavorings. Sprinkle half of the vanilla
crumbs in 12-14 muffin paper cups. Fill with chocolate mixture.
Freeze overnight.

WHEN READY TO SERVE - Sprinkle remaining crumbs or chocolate
shavings or pieces of crushed peppermint stick candy on top.

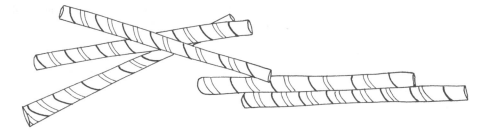

GRAHAM CRACKER PUDDING

Serves 8-10

    1/2 lb. graham crackers, crushed
    1/2 lb. marshmallows, cut fine
    1 Cup walnuts, chopped
    1 Cup dates, chopped
    1 Cup thin cream

Mix together graham crackers - rolled fine, marshmallows, nuts and
dates. Add cream slowly until mixture is moist enough to form
into a roll. Wrap in waxed paper and place in refrigerator
overnight. To keep longer place in freezer.

WHEN READY TO SERVE - Slice thin and serve with whipped cream,
custard sauce or ice cream.

Nice to have on hand for a dessert when needed.

ICEBOX CAKE

Serves 6-8

    1 lb. vanilla wafers, rolled fine
    1/4 lb. butter
    1 Cup sugar
    4 eggs
    1/4 Cup strong coffee
    1 Cup nuts, ground

Cream butter with wafers and sugar. Add eggs, one at a time.
Beat until smooth, for about 5 minutes. Mix coffee and nuts.
In a buttered dish layer crumbs and mixture. Repeat until full.
Sprinkle crumbs on top. Cover and chill in refrigerator
overnight.

WHEN READY TO SERVE - Serve with whipped cream.

Very good.

LADY LUCK PIE

Serves 6-8

    3 egg whites
    1/8 tsp. cream of tartar
    1/8 tsp. salt
    1 Cup granulated sugar
    3/4 Cups powdered sugar
    1 tsp. vanilla
    21 Ritz crackers, crushed
    1 1/4 Cups pecans, chopped
    1 (8 oz.) pkg. cream cheese, softened
    1 Cup whipping cream
    1 (7 oz.) can crushed pineapple, well drained

Preheat oven to 350°. Beat egg whites with cream of tartar and
salt. Beat until whites hold soft peaks. Add sugar gradually,
beating after each addition. Add vanilla and fold in cracker
crumbs and one half of the pecans. Press into a 9" greased pie
plate, building up sides to make crust. Bake for 20 minutes and
chill.

Beat cream cheese and powdered sugar together. Spread on crust
and chill again. Whip cream, fold in pineapple and remaining
pecans. Spread over cream cheese mixture. Cover and chill
overnight and it will be ready for a perfect dessert for any meal.

LEMON CHEESE CAKE

Serves 10-12

       1/2 Cup butter, melted
       3/4 Cup sugar
       2 Cups Zwieback crackers, rolled fine
       1 tsp. cinnamon
       2 Tbsp. gelatin
       1 Cup cold water
       3 eggs, separated
       2 Cups cream cheese
       3 Tbsp. lemon juice
       1 Tbsp. lemon rind, grated
       1/4 tsp. salt
       1/2 Cup whipping cream

Cream butter with one half of the sugar, crumbs and cinnamon.
Press 3/4's of this mixture into the bottom of a buttered 9"
spring form pan. Soak gelatin in 1/2 Cup cold water for 5
minutes. In a double boiler, cook egg yolks, remaining sugar and
1/2 Cup water. Stir constantly until mixture coats a metal spoon.
Add gelatin and stir until dissolved. Gradually add cream cheese.
Add lemon juice, rind and salt. Beat to congeal. Beat several
minutes with a beater. Whip cream. Fold cream in with stiffly
beaten egg whites and blend thoroughly. Pour mixture onto crumbs
and top with remaining crumbs. Cover and chill overnight.

This old fashioned recipe is one of our family favorites.

LEMON JELL-O CAKE

Serves 8

        1 pkg. yellow cake mix
        1 (3 oz.) box lemon Jell-O
        3/4 Cup oil
        3/4 Cup water
        4 eggs

Mix together all ingredients and beat for 4 minutes. In a greased
bundt or Angel Food cake pan, bake for 40 minutes in a 325° oven.
While still warm, poke holes in cake with fork and pour on
glaze.

Glaze: 2 Cups powdered sugar
                Juice of two lemons

Let stand overnight before serving for best flavor.

LEMON SQUARES

Serves 6-8

Crust: 1/2 Cup powdered sugar
                1 Cup butter
                2 Cups flour

Cut butter into flour and sugar. Press into a 9" x 12" pan. Bake
for 20-25 minutes in a 350° oven. Set aside.

Filling: 4 eggs, beaten
                4 Tbsp. lemon juice
                2 Cups sugar
                Rind from two lemons

Beat eggs and sugar until smooth. Gradually add lemon juice and
beat until creamy. Add lemon rind and pour over hot crust and
bake for 20-25 minutes in a 350° oven. Cover and refrigerate
overnight.

WHEN READY TO SERVE - Cut into squares.

LEMON REFRIGERATOR DESSERT

Serves 12-15

     1 1/2 pkgs. unflavored gelatin
        Dissolve in 1/2 Cup cold water
     6 eggs, separated
     1 1/2 Cups sugar, divided
     3/4 Cup lemon juice
     1 tsp. lemon peel, grated
     3/4 tsp. salt
     2 pkgs. lady fingers
     1/2 pint heavy cream, whipped
     flaked coconut

Soften gelatin in water. Beat egg yolks with 3/4 cups sugar in
the top of a double boiler. Blend in lemon juice and peel. Cook
over boiling water, stirring constantly until mixture coats a
spoon. Remove from heat and gradually stir in gelatin. Beat egg
whites until fluffy. Gradually beat in 3/4 cups sugar and until
very stiff. Fold into lemon mixture. Line a 9" x 13" or larger
glass dish with split lady fingers. Pour one half of lemon
mixture over lady fingers and cover with remaining lady fingers.
Top with remaining lemon mixture. Cover and refrigerate
overnight.

WHEN READY TO SERVE - Top with whipped cream and coconut.

MANDARIN ORANGE CAKE

Serves 12

    1 pkg. yellow cake mix
    1 small can Mandarin orange slices
    5 whole eggs
    1/2 Cup oil

Mix ingredients thoroughly. Beat at medium speed for 2 minutes.
Pour into a greased 9" x 13" cake pan and follow instruction on
cake mix box. After baking, let cake cool. Remove from pan.
Lengthwise, slice with a piece of thread the cake into 3 sections.
Apply frosting between the layers, sides and top.

Frosting: 2-3 (8 oz.) cartons whipped topping
                 1 (8 oz.) can crushed pineapple, drained
                 1 small pkg. instant vanilla pudding

Combine thoroughly and whip until smooth.

Cover cake and chill in refrigerator overnight to improve the
flavor.

OVERNIGHT MERINGUES

Serves 6-8

    1/2 Cup egg whites (3 to 4 eggs)
    3/4 Cup sugar, sifted
    1/8 tsp. salt
    1/4 tsp. cream of tartar
    1/4 tsp. vanilla

Beat egg whites with salt and cream of tartar until they peak but
not until they are dry. Add sugar while continually beating.
Blend in vanilla. Place in a lightly greased pie pan, tart pan or
kisses on a cookie sheet.

Heat oven to 350°. Turn off the heat at once after setting pans
in oven and DO NOT OPEN the oven door until oven is cold.
Suggestion: Put the meringues in the oven in the evening and let
them stay in oven overnight.

WHEN READY TO SERVE - Serve with fruit and whipped cream or ice
cream.

FOUR DECKER MOCHA

Serves 12

Crust: 1/2 Cup butter or margarine
                  1 Cup flour
                  1 Cup nuts, chopped

Mix together thoroughly and press into a buttered 9" x 13" pan.
Bake for 20 minutes in a 250° oven. Cool and set aside.

Filling: 1 (8 oz.) pkg. cream cheese
                  1 Cup powdered sugar
                  1 (16 oz.) carton whipped topping

Beat cream cheese until fluffy. Add sugar and whipped topping.
Spread into bottom of pie crust.

Filling: 1 (3 oz.) pkg. instant chocolate pudding mix
                  1 (3 oz.) pkg. instant vanilla pudding mix
                  1/8 Cup instant coffee
                  3 Cups milk

Thoroughly mix together and pour into pie crust. Top with whipped
topping. Sprinkle with nuts and grated chocolate. Cover and
refrigerate overnight. This recipe can be frozen.

MUD PIE

Serves 6-8

                  1 quart coffee ice cream, softened
                  1 (8 oz.) jar fudge topping

Crust: 24 Oreo cookies, rolled fine
                  1/3 cube butter, melted

Mix together. Press mixture into a 9" or 10" pie pan, covering
all surfaces to make a crust. Set aside.

Spread ice cream into pie crust. Cover and freeze overnight.

THE NEXT DAY: Spread fudge topping over top of ice cream. Cover
and freeze overnight.

WHEN READY TO SERVE - Garnish with whipped cream and shaved
chocolate or top with a little Kahlua.

NOODLE KUGEL

Serves 6

        1/2 lb. wide lasagna noodles, cooked
        4 eggs
        1 Cup small-curd cottage cheese
        1 Cup sour cream
        1/4 Cup butter, melted
        1 1/2 Cups milk
        1 tsp. vanilla
        3/4 Cup raisins
        1 Cup whipped cream (garnish)

Beat together eggs, sugar, cottage cheese, sour cream, butter,
milk and vanilla. Beat until smooth and well blended. In a
greased 2 to 2 1/2-quart baking dish spread 1 cup of the mixture
on the bottom. Top mixture with 1/3 of the noodles and sprinkle
with 1/4 cup of raisins. Repeat layers twice. Cover and chill
overnight in the refrigerator.

Streusel: 1/2 Cup flour
                 1/4 Cup brown sugar
                 1/2 tsp. cinnamon
                 1/4 Cup butter

Mix together flour, brown sugar and cinnamon. Cream flour mixture
with butter until coarse crumbs form. Sprinkle over the noodles
and bake uncovered in a 350° oven for 1 hour or until firm in
center.

WHEN READY TO SERVE - Cut into squares and serve with a dollop of
whipped cream on top.

OLD FASHIONED RAISIN CAKE

Serves 12

        1 Cup raisins
        3 Cups water
        2 1/2 Cups flour
        1 tsp. soda
        1 Cup sugar
        1 heaping Tbsp. shortening
        1 tsp. cinnamon
        1/2 tsp. cloves
        1/2 tsp. nutmeg

Boil water and raisins and reduce to 1 cup of liquid. Remove
raisins from liquid. Mix together raisins and 1/2 cup flour.
Mix together remaining flour and soda. Add to raisin liquid
alternating between wet and dry mixtures. Add remaining
ingredients and pour into a greased 9" square pan. Bake for 40
minutes in a 375° oven. Remove from oven. Frost with your
favorite powdered sugar frosting. Cover and refrigerate
overnight. Best to make a day ahead so flavors will blend.

This is such a favorite with my family, I _always_ double the
recipe.

ORANGE ANGEL CAKE

Serves 8-12

    1 Angel Food cake, cut in half horizontally
    1/2 Cup orange juice

Pierce cake with fork on all sides and pour orange juice over
cake.

Frosting: 3 Cups sour cream
                 6 Tbsp. confectioners sugar
                 4 Tbsp. orange juice or Cointreau
                 2 Tbsp. orange rind, grated

Thoroughly combine and spread mixture evenly between bottom layer,
sides and top of cake. As a garnish, sprinkle 1 tsp. grated
orange rind on top and sides. Cover and refrigerate overnight.
This recipe can be frozen.

FROSTY PEAR SQUARES

Serves 8

    1 (40 oz.) carton whipped cream cheese
    1/2 Cup sour cream
    1/2 (6 oz.) can frozen lemonade concentrate
    2 Tbsp. sugar
    Few drops of green food coloring
    1/2 Cup whipping cream
    1 large can pears, drained and diced
    1/2 Cup coconut

Blend together cream cheese, sour cream, lemonade concentrate,
sugar and food coloring. Add pears and coconut. Whip cream until
stiff and fold into mixture. Spread into an 8" x 8" 2" buttered
pan. Cover and refrigerate overnight.

PINEAPPLE DELIGHT

                                                         Serves 12

Crust: 2 1/2 Cups flour
                 2 cubes butter or margarine, softened
                 1/2 Cup sugar
                 1 egg, beaten

Blend flour and butter. Beat until smooth. Add sugar and egg.
Press mixture onto an ungreased cookie sheet. Bake for 20 minutes
at 350°. Cool.

Filling: 2 (3 oz.) pkgs. vanilla pudding mix
                 3 1/2 Cups milk
                 1 (20 oz.) can crushed pineapple, drained
                 1 large carton whipped topping
                 Nuts, chopped

Make pudding according to package and cook until thick. Cool.
Add pineapple. Pour over crust. Spread whipped topping on top
and sprinkle with nuts. Cover and refrigerate overnight.

WHEN READY TO SERVE - Cut into squares.

PECAN PARTY BARS

                                                         Serves 12

        1 1/2 Cups graham crackers, crushed
        1 (6 oz.) pkg. caramel or chocolate chips
        1 (3 1/2 oz.) can coconut
        1 can Eagle Brand milk
        1/2 Cup butter or margarine
        1 Cup pecans, chopped

Preheat oven to 350° or 325° for a glass dish. Melt butter in a
9" x 13" pan in the oven. Sprinkle graham cracker crumbs over
butter and pour condensed milk on top. Top with remaining
ingredients. Press down firmly. Bake for 25-30 minutes or until
lightly browned. Cover and chill in the refrigerator overnight.

WHEN READY TO SERVE - Cut into bars and serve at room temperature.
Store in the refrigerator wrapped in plastic wrap.

PINEAPPLE REFRIGERATOR CAKE

Serves 6

        1 pkg. yellow cake mix
        1 large can crushed pineapple, undrained
        1 Cup milk
        1 (8 oz.) pkg. cream cheese, softened
        1 (3 oz.) pkg. vanilla pudding mix
        1 (8 oz.) carton whipped topping
        Nuts, chopped

Make cake mix according to package. Makes holes in cake with
toothpick and pour over pineapple. Cover and refrigerate until
cooled.

When cooled, mix together milk and cream cheese. Whip until
smooth. Add vanilla pudding mix and beat until smooth. Spread
mixture over cake. Top with whipped topping and sprinkle with
nuts. Cover and refrigerate overnight.

PINEAPPLE MERINGUE CAKE

Serves 6

        8 egg whites, beaten stiff
        2 Cups sugar
        1 Tbsp. vinegar
        Pinch of salt
        1 tsp. vanilla

Line 2 - 8" layer cake pans with brown paper. While beating egg
whites, gradually add sugar. Beat until stiff. Add remaining
ingredients, folding lightly into stiffly beaten egg whites. Bake
1 to 1 1/2 hours in a very slow oven, about 300°. Peel off brown
paper from meringue immediately and let cool.

Filling: 1 small can crushed pineapple, drained
                 1 pint whipping cream, whipped until stiff

Mix together and fill between meringue layers and spread over top.
Cover and refrigerate overnight.

This was always a Woodward favorite for birthdays, etc.

PISTACHIO PIE

Serves 6

    1 prepared graham cracker crust
    1 pint pistachio ice cream, softened
    1/2 Cup milk
    1 small pkg. vanilla pudding mix
    1/2 pint whipping cream, whipped
    Nuts, chopped (topping)

Beat ice cream, milk and pudding mix together. Pour into crust
and top with whipped cream. Sprinkle with nuts. Cover and
refrigerate overnight.

PUMPKIN PIE CAKE

Serves 12-15

    1 large can pumpkin
    3 eggs, beaten
    1 large can evaporated milk
    1 Cup sugar
    3 tsp. pumpkin pie spice
      or 2 tsp. cinnamon, 1 tsp. ginger and 1/4 tsp. cloves
    1 Cup nuts, chopped
    1 cube butter, melted
    1 pkg. yellow cake mix
    1/2 pint whipping cream, whipped

Mix together pumpkin, eggs, milk, sugar and spice. Pour into a
greased 13" x 9" baking pan. Sprinkle nuts on top and drizzle
melted butter. Sprinkle cake mix over pumpkin mixture. Bake for
1 hour in a 325° oven. Cover and chill overnight in the
refrigerator.

WHEN READY TO SERVE - Top with whipped cream.

-53-

PRUNE CAKE

Serves 10-12

        1 Cup sugar
        3/4 Cup shortening
        1/2 Cup sour cream
        1 tsp. soda
        3 eggs
        2 Cups cake flour
        1 tsp. salt
        1 tsp. cinnamon
        1 tsp. allspice
        1 tsp. nutmeg
        1 Cup prunes, mashed

Cream butter and sugar. Add eggs, one at a time. Beat well. Add
sour cream and soda. Add flour and spices. Add prunes. Mix
well. Pour into 2 buttered 8" cake pans. Bake for 35 minutes in
a 375° oven. Cool and set aside.

Filling: 1/2 Cup sour cream
                1 egg
                1/2 Cup sugar
                1/2 Cup raisins
                1 Cup nuts, chopped

Mix together over low heat and stir until thick.

Icing: 2 squares chocolate
                1 Tbsp. butter
                5 Tbsp. Pet milk
                Enough sifted powdered sugar until consistency
                  spreads well

This cake is best made a day ahead allowing flavors to blend.

QUEEN'S CAKE
                                                   Serves 10-12

        1 Cup sugar
        6 Tbsp. butter
        1 egg
        1/2 Cup walnuts, chopped
        1 1/4 Cups flour
        1 tsp. baking powder
        1/2 tsp. salt

Mix together thoroughly. Pour into a greased 9" square pan. Bake
for 45 minutes in a 350° oven. Cool and set aside.

Frosting: 5 Tbsp. brown sugar
                  2 Tbsp. butter
                  2 Tbsp. cream
                  Walnuts, whole (topping)

Mix together and bring to a boil. Boil for 3 minutes and beat
until mixture turns to fudge. Pour over cake and top with whole
walnuts.

This cake is best kept overnight before serving.

RASPBERRY RUM MOUSSE

Serves 6-8

    1 can raspberries
    2/3 Cup water
    1/3 Cup rum
    1 small pkg. raspberry Jell-O
    1 Cup whipping cream, whipped
    16 marshmallows, cut up

Drain raspberries and retain juice. Combine 1 cup of raspberry
juice, water and rum. Bring to a boil. Add marshmallows. Stir
until dissolved. In a bowl add mixture and add Jell-O, stirring
constantly. Chill until fairly well set. When thick fold in
raspberries and whipped cream. Pour mousse into a lightly oiled
mold and chill overnight covered.

REFRIGERATOR COOKIES

3-4 dozen

    1 Cup shortening (part margarine)
    1 Cup sugar
    2 eggs
    1 1/2 tsp. vanilla
    3 Cups flour
    1 tsp. salt
    1/2 tsp. soda
    Colored sugar or nonpareils

Mix together sugar, eggs and vanilla. Beat until smooth. Mix
together flour, salt and soda. Blend into eggs and sugar mixture.
Mix thoroughly with hands. Divide into 3 parts and shape into
rolls 1 1/2" in diameter and 7" long. Roll in colored sugar or
nonpareils. Cover with plastic wrap and chill overnight in the
refrigerator.

WHEN READY TO SERVE - Cut into 1/4" thick slices and bake for 8-10
minutes in 400° oven.

These are nice to have on hand for a quick dessert.

SNOWBALLS

Serves 12-16

    1 Cup sugar
    1/2 Cup butter
    2 eggs, separated
    1 Cup crushed pineapple, drained
    1 Cup walnuts, finely chopped
    2 pkgs. lemon wafers

Cream sugar and butter. Add slightly beaten egg yolks to mixture and beat. Add walnuts and crushed pineapple and mix well. Beat egg whites until stiff and fold into creamed mixture. Alternating wafers, place 1 tsp. filling, making a four high cookie stack. Cover and chill overnight.

WHEN READY TO SERVE - Frost with 1 pint whipping cream, whipped and rolled into tinted coconut.

This is a very nice dessert for a shower or ladies luncheon.

STRAWBERRY DELIGHT

Serves 12-16

    1 Angel Food cake
    4 (3 oz.) pkgs. strawberry Jell-O
      Dissolve in 2 Cups boiling water
    2 pkgs. frozen strawberries
    1/2 pint whipping cream, whipped

Add strawberries to dissolved Jell-O and stir until thick. Break cake into small pieces. Mix cake together with Jell-O mixture, making sure cake is well covered. Cover and refrigerate overnight.

WHEN READY TO SERVE - Serve with whipped cream.

FROSTY STRAWBERRY SQUARES

Serves 12

        1 Cup flour
        1/4 Cup brown sugar
        1/2 Cup nuts, chopped
        1/2 Cup butter, melted

Mix ingredients together and pour into a lightly oiled 9" x 13"
pan. Bake for 20 minutes in a 350° oven, stirring occasionally.
Cool and save 1 cup for topping.

Topping: 2 Cups sliced strawberries, fresh or frozen
                 2 Tbsp. lemon juice
                 2 egg whites
                 1 Cup sugar
                 1 carton whipped topping

At high speed, beat strawberries, lemon juice, egg whites and
sugar for 10 minutes. Beat until peaks form. Fold in whipped
topping. Spread into pan over baked crumbs. Top with reserved
crumbs. Cover and freeze overnight.

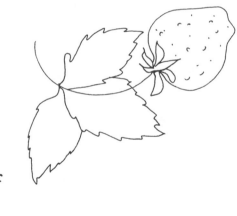

SUGAR COOKIE PIZZA

Serves 8-10

        1 Cup sugar
        1 Cup powdered sugar
        1 Cup margarine
        1 Cup vegetable oil
        4 Cups flour
        1 tsp. cream of tartar
        1 tsp. soda
        2 eggs
        1 tsp. vanilla
        1/2 pint whipped topping (topping)

Mix together ingredients. Pour into a greased quiche pan forming
a crust and bake for 10-12 minutes in a 350° oven. Top with
pudding, fresh fruit and whipped cream.

TOPPING SUGGESTIONS: Pudding, fresh fruit, whipped cream.

SWEDISH TORTE

Serves 6-8

        3 eggs
        1 Cup sugar
        1 Cup graham crackers crumbs (not too fine)
        1/2 Cup walnuts, chopped
        1 tsp. vanilla
        Pinch of salt
        1/2 pint whipping cream, whipped

Beat eggs with an electric mixer until very light. Add sugar and
beat until mixed. Excluding whipping cream, fold in remaining
ingredients and pour into a buttered 9" pie pan. Bake for 30
minutes in a 350° oven. Cool and cover torte completely with
whipped cream. Cover and refrigerate overnight.

A very light delicious dessert after a company dinner.

SWEET POTATO ICEBOX COOKIES

4 dozen

        4 sweet potatoes (cooked and mashed)
        1 1/2 Cups shortening
        1/3 Cup white sugar
        1/2 tsp. soda
        2 tsp. cinnamon
        2 tsp. baking powder
        1 Cup brown sugar
        3 eggs
        1 tsp. salt
        4 Cups flour
        1/2 Cup nuts, chopped
        1/2 Cup raisins

Cream shortening and sugars and beat well. Add eggs, one egg at a
time and beat again. Set aside. Sift flour and other dry
ingredients together. Add to egg and sugar mixture. Add nuts,
raisins and sweet potatoes. Roll into sausage-like rolls. Wrap
in waxed paper and place in refrigerator overnight.

WHEN READY TO SERVE - Slice into very thin slices. Bake on a
cookie sheet in a very hot oven, 400° for 8-10 minutes.

Store in a covered container.

TIA MARIA MOUSSE

Serves 8-10

      6 egg yolks
      3/4 Cup sugar
      1 1/2 Cups strong coffee
      2 pkgs. unflavored gelatin
      1 1/2 pints whipping cream, whipped

Mix together egg yolks, sugar and coffee. Cook in a double boiler
until mixture is a soft custard. Fold in whipped cream. Pour
into a lightly oiled 2-quart mold. Cover and chill overnight in
the refrigerator.

Sauce: 3 Cups strong coffee
                1 1/2 Cups sugar
                2 Tbsp. cornstarch
                1/4 Cup water, cold
                2 oz. Tia Maria or Kahlua

Heat coffee with sugar. Mix together cornstarch and water and
blend with sweet coffee mixture. Simmer and stir until liquid
thickens. Add liqueur.

WHEN READY TO SERVE - Pour sauce over mousse.

TORTILLA TORTE

Serves 8

      4 - 7" flour tortillas
      6 oz. chocolate chips, melted
      2 Cups sour cream
      2 Tbsp. powdered sugar

Mix together chocolate, 1 Cup sour cream and 1 Tbsp. sugar over
hot water. Let cool. Spread cooled chocolate mixture on top of
each tortilla. Form a stack by placing tortillas on top of each
other. End with tortilla on top. Mix together remaining sour
cream and sugar. Spread mixture over entire stack. Cover and
refrigerate overnight.

WHEN READY TO SERVE - Top with shaved milk chocolate and cut into
pie wedges when serving.

TRIFLE
                                                        Serves 10-12

    1 1/2 lb. pound cake or sponge loaf cakes

    1 large pkg. vanilla pudding mix, prepared and
      cooled but not set

    1 (10 oz.) frozen strawberries, thawed - retain liquid
    1 (10 oz.) frozen raspberries, thawed - retain liquid
    1 (10 oz.) frozen mixed fruit, thawed and drained
    3/4 Cup light rum
    5 bananas, sliced
    1/2 pint whipping cream (topping)
    2 tsp. sugar
    Coconut (topping)
    Slivered almonds (topping)
    Maraschino cherries (topping)

Slice cake and fit pieces into the bottom of a trifle bowl. Mash
strawberries and raspberries together. Mix mashed berries with
rum and berry juices. Over the top of cake in trifle bowl, layer
bananas, mixed fruit, mashed berries and prepared pudding mix.
Repeating layers with pudding on top. Cover and refrigerate
overnight.

WHEN READY TO SERVE - Whip whipping cream with sugar. Spread on
top. Garnish trifle with coconut, almonds and cherries.

WALNUT ICEBOX COOKIES

2 dozen

    1 lb. margarine
    1 Cup brown sugar
    1 Cup white sugar
    1 tsp. baking soda
    2 eggs
    1 Cup walnuts, chopped
    5 Cups flour

Mix all ingredients together and form into rolls. Cover with plastic wrap and refrigerate overnight.

WHEN READY TO SERVE - Slice rolls into thin slices and bake on a cookie sheet for 8-10 minutes in a 400° oven.

Handy to have in the refrigerator, to bake when needed.

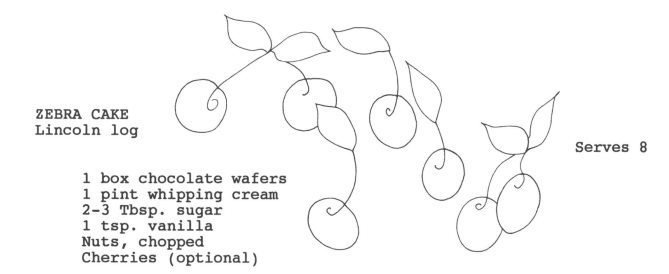

ZEBRA CAKE
Lincoln log

Serves 8

    1 box chocolate wafers
    1 pint whipping cream
    2-3 Tbsp. sugar
    1 tsp. vanilla
    Nuts, chopped
    Cherries (optional)

Whip cream until stiff and sweetened with sugar and vanilla. Spread whipped cream mixture between cookies forming a log as you go. Frost complete log with whipped cream. Cover and refrigerate overnight.

WHEN READY TO SERVE - Garnish with chopped nuts and cherries and cut diagonally.

A nice party dessert, this is easy to make and looks so fancy when served.

Entrees

BAR-B-Q-BEEF

    4 lb. beef clod roast
    2 Tbsp. white vinegar
    1 tsp. pepper
    1 tsp. salt
    1 medium onion, chopped
    2 Tbsp. Worcestershire sauce
    1 tsp. paprika
    2 (8 oz.) cans tomato sauce
    1 (6 oz.) can tomato paste
    4 oz. ketchup
    2 Cups water
    8-10 French rolls (for serving)

Place beef roast in heavy covered pot. Mix rest of ingredients
together and pour over roast. Bring to boil. Cover and simmer
over medium heat for 2 hours. Cool meat and shred.

This can be made a day ahead of serving. Refrigerate.

WHEN READY TO SERVE - Warm and serve on French rolls, cut in half.
Makes 8 generous servings.

BEEF BURRITOS

    1 pkg. flour tortillas
    5 lbs. round steak
    1 lb. lean pork steak
    2 medium onions, chopped
    1 medium can tomatoes
    1 small can green chilies, diced
    Dash of corn starch
    Salt and pepper to taste

Cut meat into strips and brown. Add remaining ingredients and
bring to boil. Turn heat down, cover and simmer for 3 to 4 hours.

This is best made a day ahead and then warmed and served in large
flour tortillas the next day.

BEEF AND CORN LOAF

Serves 8

        1 lb. lean ground round
        1/2 lb. lean ground pork
        2 eggs
        1 small onion, finely chopped
        1/2 Cup green pepper, finely chopped
        1 (8 oz.) can cream style corn
        2/3 Cups yellow cornmeal
        1 1/2 tsp. salt
        1 1/2 tsp. pepper
        1 pkg. beef gravy mix

Reserve beef gravy and mix together rest of ingredients. Press
mixture loosely into 5" x 9" loaf pan. Cover and refrigerate
overnight.

Prepare beef gravy mix according to package directions. Pour over
top of meat loaf. Bake at 350° for 1 to 1 1/2 hours. Cut into
slices and serve hot.

BEEF FRITOLI CASSEROLE

Serves 6

        3 Cups corn chips
        1 lb. ground chuck
        1/4 Cup minced onion
        1 (15 oz.) can chili beans
        1 (4 oz.) can sliced olives
        1 Tbsp. water
        1/2 tsp. salt
        1 1/2 Cups sharp cheddar cheese, grated

Place 2 Cups corn chips in 1 1/2 quart casserole. Brown meat with
onion in skillet, stirring to keep meat crumbly. Add undrained
beans and olives, water, salt and 3/4 cups of cheese. Mix well
and spread over chips in casserole. Cover and refrigerate
overnight. Before serving, sprinkle remaining chips and cheese
over top. Cover and bake at 350° for 30 minutes. To brown,
uncover and cook for 10 more minutes.

ITALIAN BEEF

Serves 6

    4 lbs. rump, sirloin tip or heel of round roast
    1 can beef bouillon
    1 pkg. onion soup mix
    1 tsp. garlic powder or garlic salt
    1 tsp. oregano

Cook roast slowly in crockpot in beef bouillon until tender. Add
other ingredients. Cook 1 to 2 hours more. Add water when
needed. It is best when roast falls apart.

Make a day ahead and use for French dip sandwiches or over noodles
or rice.

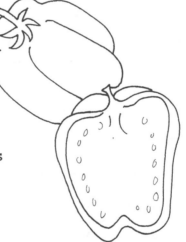

STUFFED BELL PEPPERS

Serves 6

    6 Bell peppers, cored
    1 lb. ground round
    1 onion, chopped
    1 (14 1/2 oz.) can tomatoes
    1 can water
    1/2 can corn (10 1/2 oz.)
    1 pkg. taco seasoning mix
    1 1/2 Cups rice
    2 Tbsp. sugar
    1 can tomato soup
    Salt and pepper to taste

Brown ground round with onion. Add tomatoes, corn, taco mix
water, rice, sugar, salt and pepper. Bring to a boil. Reduce
heat to low and cover. Simmer for 20-25 minutes, until rice is
done.

Stuff peppers and arrange in low baking dish. Cover with tomato
soup. Cover with foil and refrigerate overnight.

WHEN READY TO SERVE - Cook uncovered at 350° for 30 to 45 minutes
until hot and brown on top.....Yummy!

CREAMED CHICKEN

Serves 4-6

    1/4 Cup butter or margarine, melted
    1/4 Cup carrot, grated
    1/4 Cup celery, diced
    1/4 Cup green onion, diced
    1/4 Cup flour
    1 Cup chicken broth
    1 Cup milk
    2 Cups chicken or turkey, cooked and diced
    1 (2 1/2 oz.) jar sliced mushrooms
    1/4 Cup pimento, chopped
    Parsley sprigs (garnish)

Mix butter and flour together. In a sauce pan, over low heat, add
chicken broth and milk and stir until thickened. Add remaining
ingredients and cook until vegetables are tender.

When making a day ahead, place in casserole, cover and chill in
refrigerator overnight.

WHEN READY TO SERVE THE NEXT DAY - Bake casserole in 350° oven for
30 minutes or until thoroughly warmed and serve over party shells,
rice or noodles. Garnish with parsley sprigs.

CHICKEN AND DRESSING SUPREME

Serves 6-8

    2 1/2 Cups chicken, cooked and diced
    1 pkg. seasoned stuffing mix
    1 can cream of chicken soup
    1 can cream of celery soup
    3 stalks celery, chopped
    2 medium onions, chopped
    2 Tbsp. butter or margarine
    1/2 can milk
    1/2 can chicken broth
    1/4 Cup slivered almonds

Saute onions, celery and almonds in 2 tablespoons of butter until
soft. Add bread stuffing mix moistened with chicken broth. In a
long flat casserole place mixture and cover with chicken. Combine
soups, milk and broth and pour over casserole. Cover with foil
and chill overnight in the refrigerator.

WHEN READY TO SERVE - Bake for 1 hour in a 350° oven or until well
browned and bubbly.

CHICKEN BREASTS DIVAN

        4 chicken breasts, split and boned
        1/4 Cup margarine
        1 tsp. paprika
        2 (10 oz.) pkgs. frozen broccoli spears, cooked and drained
        1 (10 oz.) can cream of mushroom soup
        1/2 Cup Best Foods mayonnaise
        2 tsp. lemon juice
        2 Tbsp. Parmesan cheese, grated

Steam chicken breasts before browning in margarine in large
skillet. Sprinkle salt and paprika over chicken. Place broccoli
in a greased 12" x 8" x 2" baking dish. Top with chicken.
Combine soup, mayonnaise and lemon juice and spread on top of
chicken. Cover and chill overnight in the refrigerator.

WHEN READY TO SERVE - Sprinkle cheese on top of chicken and bake
for 30 to 35 minutes in a 350° oven. The last 2 to 3 minutes
place under broiler and slightly brown top.

This is an all-time favorite for family or entertaining. Serve
with rice and salad.

CHICKEN BREASTS WITH PECAN STUFFING

Serves 8

        10 (6 oz.) chicken breasts, deboned
        1 lb. ground pork
        2 small onions, finely chopped
        1 bell pepper, finely chopped
        3 celery stalks, finely chopped
        1 Tbsp. sweet basil
        2 Tbsp. allspice
        Black and red pepper
        Salt to taste
        1/2 pint whipping cream
        1 Cup pecans, chopped finely
        1 egg
        Parsley (garnish)

Process two of the chicken breasts in a food mill or grinder and set aside. Add egg and herb seasonings to onions, celery and green pepper. Mix well into ground pork. Pound chicken breasts to the thickness of a crepe, but not breaking apart.

In the center of each breast place a thin layer of pork mixture, whipping cream, pecans and ground chicken. Roll up each breast, making sure all stuffing is well secured and place (fold side down) on a baking tin and refrigerate overnight.

WHEN READY TO SERVE - One hour before serving preheat oven to 350°
and bake for 45 minutes or until golden brown.

BAKED CHICKEN BREASTS SUPREME

Serves 12

         12 split chicken breasts
         2 Cups sour cream or cottage cheese
         1/2 Cup lemon juice,
         4 tsp. Worcestershire sauce
         4 tsp. celery salt
         2 tsp. paprika
         2 cloves garlic, crushed
         Salt and pepper to taste
         Bread crumbs
         1/2 Cup butter, melted
         1/2 Cup margarine, melted

Mix together sour cream, lemon juice, Worcestershire sauce, celery
salt, paprika, garlic salt and pepper. Coat mixture on chicken
and allow to marinate in refrigerate overnight. When ready to
bake, roll each chicken breast in breadcrumbs. Arrange chicken in
shallow baking dish (fold side down).   Melt butter and margarine
together and pour over top of chicken. Bake in an uncovered
baking dish for 40 minutes. Spoon on rest of butter mixture and
bake for an additional 20 minutes, until tender.

FOOTNOTE: Your hands will get quite messy when rolling up chicken
so it helps to have a helper add crumbs when needed.

OVERNIGHT CHICKEN CASSEROLE

Serves 6-8

        2 Cups milk
        2 (10 3/4 oz.) cans cream of mushroom soup
        1 (8 oz.) pkg. elbow macaroni
        1 (8 oz.) can water chestnuts, thinly sliced
        2 Cups chicken, diced
        1 Cup onion, chopped
        1 1/2 Cup cheddar cheese, grated
        1/4 tsp. salt
        Pepper to taste
        4 hard-cooked eggs, sliced
        1/3 Cup parsley, chopped (garnish)
        1 small jar pimento strips (garnish)

Set aside parsley, pimentos and 1 egg for garnish.

In a large bowl, combine milk and soup with remaining ingredients
to uncooked macaroni and mix well. Transfer chicken mixture to a
large buttered rectangle baking dish, 13" x 9" x 2" and cover
securely. Refrigerate overnight.

WHEN READY TO SERVE - Bake uncovered in 325° oven for 1 1/4 hours.
Garnish with egg, pimento and parsley. Serve hot.

HAWAIIAN CHICKEN

Serves 6

        6 chicken breasts, boned
          or 6 pork chops
        1 (9 oz.) can crushed pineapple
        1/2 Cup butter or margarine
        1/4 Cup brown sugar
        2 Tbsp. corn starch
        1 tsp. salt
        1/4 tsp. pepper
        1/4 Cup vinegar
        2 Tbsp. chili sauce
        1/3 Cup ketchup
        1 tsp. soy sauce
        Shredded coconut (garnish)
        Almonds, slivered (garnish)

Excluding chicken breasts, coconut and almonds, mix together
ingredients and cook on top of stove, until smooth. Arrange
chicken in a baking dish and pour mixture on top. Garnish with
nuts and coconut. Cover and refrigerate overnight.

WHEN READY TO SERVE - Allow casserole to stand at room temperature
for 15 minutes before baking for 1 hour at 325°.

MEXICAN STYLE CHICKEN KIEV

Serves 8

    8 split chicken breasts, skinned and boned
    1 (7 oz.) can diced green chilies
    4 oz. Monterey jack cheese, cut into strips
    1/2 Cup bread crumbs, fine grind
    1/2 Cup Parmesan cheese, grated
    1 Tbsp. chili powder
    1/2 tsp. salt
    1/4 tsp. ground cumin
    1/4 tsp. black pepper
    6 Tbsp. butter, melted
    1 can tomato sauce
    1 can salsa
    Bread crumbs

Pound chicken into 1/4" thick pieces. Put 2 tablespoons of
chilies and 1 strip of jack cheese in center of each chicken
piece. Roll up and tuck ends under. Combine bread crumbs with
Parmesan cheese, chili powder, salt, cumin and pepper. Dip each
stuffed chicken piece in shallow bowl containing 6 Tbsp. melted
butter and roll in crumb mixture. Place chicken rolls, seam side
down, in oblong baking dish and drizzle with a little melted
butter. Cover and chill for 4 hours or overnight.

WHEN READY TO SERVE - Bake uncovered at 400° for 30 minutes.
Serve with tomato sauce and salsa mixed.

CHICKEN NUT NOODLE CASSEROLE

Serves 6-8

    2 large cans Chow Mein noodles
    2 Cups chicken, cubed
      coarsely flaked tuna can be substituted
    1 Cup celery, diced
    1 bunch green onions, chop including tops
    2 cans cream of chicken soup
    1/2 Cup milk
    1 can sliced mushrooms, drained
    1 can water chestnuts, drained
    1/2 Cup toasted almonds
      or pecans, walnuts or cashews can be substituted

Cover bottom of greased baking dish with half of the noodles. On top of the noodles place one half of the cubed chicken. On top place one half of the onions, mushrooms and water chestnuts. Repeat with a second layer.

Thin cream of chicken soup with milk and pour over top of chicken mixture. Cover with remaining noodles and top with nuts. Cover and refrigerate overnight.

WHEN READY TO SERVE - Bake uncovered for 40 minutes in 350° oven.

OVEN CHICKEN BREASTS

Serves 6-8

    6-8 split chicken breasts
    1 can cream of mushroom soup
    1 can cream of chicken soup
    1 pkg. dry seasoned dressing
    1 cube butter, melted

Mix soups together and spread on top of chicken breasts in a 9" x 13" baking dish. Sprinkle dry dressing on top and dribble melted butter over dressing. Cover and chill overnight in the refrigerator.

WHEN READY TO SERVE - Bake uncovered for 1 hour in 350° oven.

NORDIC CHICKEN SURPRISE
                                                          Serves 6

        1/2 Cup prosciuto, chopped
        1/2 Cup fresh mushrooms, chopped
        2 Tbsp. butter or margarine
        1/3 Cup green onion, chopped
        2 Tbsp. parsley, chopped
        1 Cup shredded Jarlsberg cheese
        3 whole chicken breasts, boned, split and pounded thin
        1/3 Cup flour
        2 eggs, well beaten
        2 Tbsp. water
        3/4 Cup dry bread crumbs, fine
        3/4 tsp. salt
        1/8 tsp. pepper
        3 Tbsp. butter or margarine
        Cheese sauce (recipe below)

In a saucepan, brown prosciuto and mushrooms in 2 Tbsp. butter.
Cook onion with parsley until tender. Remove from heat. Cool
slightly and blend in cheese. Divide filling among chicken
breasts. Roll up, fully enclosing cheese mixture. Fasten with
toothpicks.

Place flour, egg mixed with water and bread crumbs seasoned with
salt and pepper in 3 separate shallow dishes. Coat chicken first
in flour, then in egg, then in bread crumbs. Cover and chill
overnight in refrigerator.

WHEN READY TO SERVE - Place in a shallow buttered baking dish.
Dot with remaining butter and bake at 375° for 35 minutes or until
golden brown. Turn once.

CHEESE SAUCE: 2 Tbsp. butter
                2 Tbsp. flour

In a sauce pan combine butter and flour and cook until bubbly.
Stir constantly. Remove from heat.

    Add: 1 1/2 Cup chicken broth

Return to heat and cook, stirring constantly until thickened and
smooth.

    Add: 1 Cup Jarlsberg cheese
                1 tsp. dry mustard
                Salt to taste

Serve over chicken and garnish with 1/8 tsp. paprika.

CHICKEN PARTY CASSEROLE

Serves 6-8

6 chicken breasts, cooked and cubed

1 lb. noodles, cooked and drained
  (Cook in boiling water with 1 chopped onion and 1 tsp.
  salt)
1/4 lb. butter
1 pint of heavy cream

1 (3 oz.) can pimentos
1/2 Cup celery, diced
1/2 Cup green onion, chopped
1 can sliced water chestnuts
1 1/2 lb. fresh mushrooms, sliced
1 Tbl. poppy seed
1/2 Cup slivered almonds
1 tsp. garlic, crushed
1/2 lb. jack or cheddar cheese, grated
1 can chicken broth
1 can cream of mushroom soup
1/2 Cup white wine
1 pkg. dry dressing mix

In a large bowl add butter and cream to noodles and add chicken.
Saute mushrooms and add to chicken mixture. Add remaining
ingredients excluding dry dressing mix and cover. Chill in
refrigerator overnight.

WHEN READY TO SERVE - Top casserole with one package of dry
dressing mix. Bake at 375° uncovered for 1 hour.

Serve with a green salad and French rolls for a fabulous party
dinner.

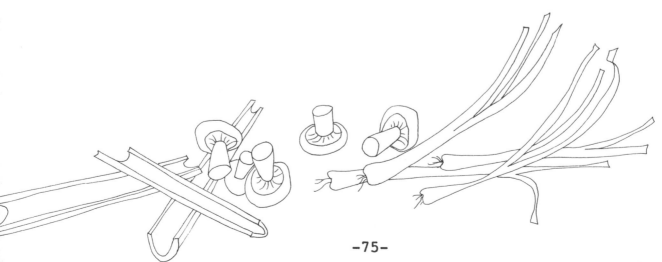

CHICKEN TORTILLA CASSEROLE

Serves 8-10

    4 whole chicken breasts
    1 dozen corn tortillas, cut into 1" strips
    1 can cream of chicken soup
    1 Cup milk
    1 onion, grated
    1/2 can green chili salsa
    1 lb. cheddar cheese, cubed
       or 1/2 lb. Monterey jack and 1/2 lb. cheddar

Wrap breasts in foil and bake at 400° for 1 hour. Bone chicken
and cut into large pieces. Mix soup, milk, onion and salsa
together. Butter shallow dish and spread a layer of tortillas on
bottom and then layer chicken. Cover with some soup mixture and
half of the cheese. Repeat layers, ending with cheese. Cover and
refrigerate overnight.

WHEN READY TO SERVE - Bake for 1 to 1 1/2 hours in 300° oven.

VARIATION: Add 12 fresh mushrooms cut into quarters, 1/4 tsp.
allspice and 1/4 tsp. nutmeg.

BAKED CHICKEN AND RICE

        2 Cups chicken, cooked and chopped
        1 Cup rice, cooked
        3 hard cooked eggs, chopped
        1 can cream of chicken soup
        2/3 cup mayonnaise
        2 Tbsp. celery, chopped
        1 Tbsp. lemon juice
        1/4 Cup water
        Salt and pepper to taste
        1/2 to 1 Cup sharp cheese
        2 Cups potato chips, crushed

Mix all ingredients together, except cheese and chips. Spread in
a lightly greased 1 1/2-quart loaf pan or a 9" x 13" baking dish.

WHEN READY TO SERVE - Cover casserole with cheese and chips and
bake at 400° for 25 minutes. This dish can be prepared ahead and
refrigerated overnight.

VARIATION: Substitute 1 cup sliced water chestnuts for the eggs
and top with 1 cup corn flakes combined with 1/2 stick of butter.

CHICKEN-WILD RICE CASSEROLE

Serves 6-8

        1 (6 oz.) pkg. long grain and wild rice
        1/4 Cup butter or margarine
        1/4 Cup all-purpose flour
        1 (13 oz.) can evaporated milk
        1/2 Cup chicken broth
        2 1/2 Cups cooked chicken, chopped
        1 (3 oz.) can sliced mushrooms, drained
        1/3 Cup green pepper, chopped
        1/4 Cup pimento, chopped
        1/4 Cup slivered almonds

Prepare rice according to package directions and set aside. Melt
butter in heavy saucepan over low heat. Add flour, stirring until
smooth. Cook for 1 minute, stirring constantly. Gradually add
milk and broth. Cook over medium heat, stirring constantly until
thickened and bubbly. Combine all ingredients, except almonds and
pour into lightly greased 2-quart casserole. Sprinkle almonds on
top, cover and refrigerate overnight.

WHEN READY TO SERVE - Let casserole stand at room temperature for
30 minutes before baking. Bake uncovered for 35 minutes in 350°
oven.

Serve with fruit salad and simple vegetable.

REAL CHILI CON CARNE

Serves 10-12

    4 lbs. beef cut fine (like hamburger)
    5 medium onions, chopped fine
    2 celery stalks, diced
    1/2 green pepper, diced
    2 cloves garlic, chopped fine
    2 Tbsp. butter or olive oil
    6 Tbsp. chili powder (more if desired)
    1 Tbsp. flour
    2 tsp. ground coriander
    2 tsp. cumin seed
    2 tsp. oregano
    2 (#2) can tomatoes
    4 Tbsp. sugar
    1 Tbsp. salt
    2 squares unsweetened chocolate (secret ingredient)
    1 can chili beans (optional)
    Parmesan cheese (condiment)

Saute onion and garlic in oil until golden brown and limp. Mix
chili powder, flour and herb seasonings together and add to onion
mixture. Cook for 3 minutes. Add tomatoes including liquid.
Cool and simmer. Add sugar, salt and chocolate. Should be
consistency of gravy and can be thinned with tomato juice.

Add beef to sauce and cook until tender. To improve add 2 cans of
chili beans. Best if refrigerated overnight.

WHEN READY TO SERVE - Reheat before serving and sprinkle with
Parmesan cheese.

CHEDDAR CHILI PIE

Serves 6

        1 lb. lean ground beef or veal
        1 large onion, chopped
          or 4 green onions, chopped
        2 cloves garlic, chopped fine
        1 (28 oz.) can tomatoes
        1 (15 oz.) can kidney beans with juice
        1 1/4 Cups cornmeal
        1 Cup cheddar cheese, grated
        2 Tbsp. chili powder
        1 tsp. cumin
        1/4 tsp. cayenne
        1/2 tsp. crushed red pepper
        1/2 tsp. black pepper
        Dash of Tabasco
        1 1/4 Cups skim milk
        Salt and pepper to taste

Saute beef, onion and garlic together until brown. Drain off fat.
Add tomatoes, beans, 3/4 cups cornmeal, 1/2 Cup cheese and
seasonings. Cook over low heat, stirring occasionally for about
15 minutes. Pour mixture into a casserole.

In the same sauce pan, combine milk, remaining cornmeal, salt and
pepper to taste. Stir over low heat until thickened. Add the
remaining cheese and eggs. Stir until smooth. Pour over meat
mixture. Refrigerate overnight.

Bake uncovered at 375° for 30 minutes or until crust is lightly
browned.

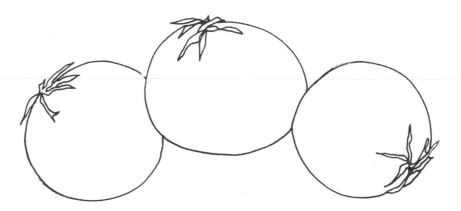

CHILI RELLENOS CASSEROLE
                                                    Serves 6

        1 lb. ground beef
        1/2 Cup onion, chopped
        1/2 tsp. salt
        1/4 tsp. pepper
        2 (4 oz.) cans whole green chilies, cut lengthwise and seeded
        1 1/2 Cups (6 oz.) medium cheddar cheese, grated
        1/4 Cup all-purpose flour
        4 eggs, beaten
        1 1/2 Cups milk
        4 dashes of hot sauce
        1/2 tsp. salt
        Dash of pepper

Brown ground beef with onion until crumbled. Add salt and pepper
and set aside.

Arrange half of the chilies in a lightly greased, 10" x 6" x 1
1/2" baking dish. Sprinkle cheese on top of chilies, add meat
mixture and top with remaining chilies.

Combine flour with 1/4 Cup milk to make a smooth mixture. Add
eggs, remaining milk and seasonings. Pour over casserole. Cover
and refrigerate overnight.

WHEN READY TO SERVE - Bake at 350° for 50 minutes. Let stand for
5 minutes before serving. Cut into squares.

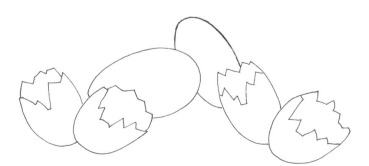

CHOP SUEY

Serves 6

    1 1/2 lb. lean pork, cut into small pieces
    4 good sized onions, sliced
    2 Cups celery, chopped
    1/2 lb. fresh mushrooms, sliced
    2 Tbsp. dark molasses
    2 Tbsp. soy sauce
    1/2 Cup water

RESERVE:

    3 Cups rice, cooked
    2 Cups bean sprouts
    1 Tbsp. vegetable oil

Quickly fry pork and set aside. Add water, vegetables and
seasonings and cook until tender. Cover and refrigerate
overnight.

WHEN READY TO SERVE - Saute 2 cups bean sprouts quickly in
vegetable oil. Add other mixture and cook for a few minutes.
Serve hot over rice.

COMPANY CASSEROLE WITH NOODLES

Serves 6-8

    4 Cups noodles (1/2 lb.)
    1 lb. ground beef
    2 (8 oz.) cans tomato sauce
    1 Cup cottage cheese
    1 (8 oz.) pkg. cream cheese, softened
    1/4 Cup sour cream
    1/3 Cup onion, minced
    1 Tbsp. green onion, minced

Early in the day: Cook noodles according to package directions.
Drain and set aside. Saute beef until brown. Stir in tomato
sauce. Remove from heat. Combine cottage cheese and remaining
ingredients.

In a 2-quart casserole spread half of noodles and cover with
cheese mixture. Add the remaining noodles and cover with tomato
meat mixture. Cover and refrigerate overnight.

WHEN READY TO SERVE - Bake for 30 minutes at 350°.

Best served with tossed green salad and garlic bread.

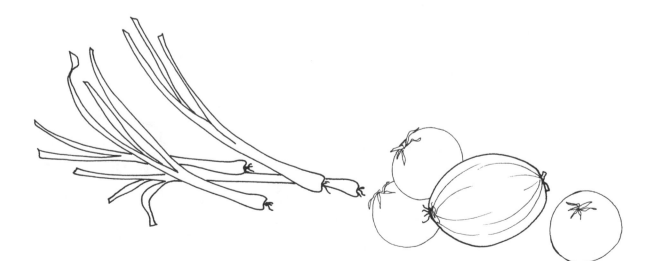

CRAB SOUFFLE

Serves 6

    8 slices white bread
    2 cans crab meat
    1 onion, chopped
    1/2 Bell pepper, chopped
    1 Cup celery, chopped
    1/2 Cup mayonnaise
    3 Cups milk
    4 eggs, beaten
    1 can cream of mushroom soup
    1/2 Cup cheese, grated
    1/2 tsp. paprika
    Salt and pepper to taste

Dice 4 slices of bread into baking dish. Mix together crabmeat, mayonnaise, onion, green pepper and celery. Place on top of prepared bread. Trim crusts on 4 remaining slices of bread and place on top of mixture. Mix eggs and milk together and pour over prepared casserole. Cover and refrigerate overnight.

WHEN READY TO SERVE - Bake 15 minutes at 325°. Take from oven and spread soup on top. Top with cheese and paprika. Return to oven and bake again for 1 hour.

CRABMEAT-BROCCOLI CASSEROLE

Serves 8

        1 lb. crabmeat
        12 slices bread
        2 1/2 Cups milk
        1 Cup mayonnaise
        7 hard-cooked eggs, finely chopped
        1/4 lb. onion, chopped
        1 Tbsp. + 1 tsp. parsley, minced
        2 (10 oz.) pkgs. frozen broccoli
        1 Cup sharp cheddar cheese, grated

Remove crust from bread. Cut bread into 1/2" cubes. Combine bread cubes, milk and mayonnaise. Stir well. Cover and refrigerate for 30 minutes. Remove mixture from refrigerator and stir in eggs, crabmeat, onion and parsley.

Barely cook broccoli. Drain well. Arrange broccoli in a lightly greased, 13" x 9" x 2", baking dish. Spoon crabmeat mixture evenly over broccoli. Cover and refrigerate overnight.

WHEN READY TO SERVE - Bake in oven for 40 minutes in 325° oven. Sprinkle cheese on top and bake for an additional 5 minutes.

CRAB-MUSHROOM CASSEROLE

Serves 4-5

    1 (8 oz.) pkg. of noodles
    1/4 lb. fresh mushrooms, (2 cups chopped)
    6 scallions or green onions
    3/4 cube butter
    1 tsp. basil
    1 tsp. oregano
    6 cloves garlic
    Salt and white pepper to taste
    1 (8 oz.) carton of sour cream
    3/4 Cup sherry wine
    1/2 Cup heavy cream
    4 oz. crab meat
    1 Cup Provolone cheese, cut into pieces
    Romano cheese, grated (garnish)
    Parsley (garnish)

Prepare noodles according to directions. Drain and set aside.
Saute mushrooms, garlic, onions and basil in butter. Add salt and
pepper. Add wine and continue to cook for 2-3 minutes. Add sour
cream and heavy cream.

In a buttered casserole spread with bread crumbs. Place noodles,
Provolone cheese and crab in layers. Pour sauce over top and
sprinkle with Romano cheese. Cover and refrigerate overnight.

WHEN READY TO SERVE - Bake at 350° for 30-40 minutes. Garnish
with parsley and serve hot.

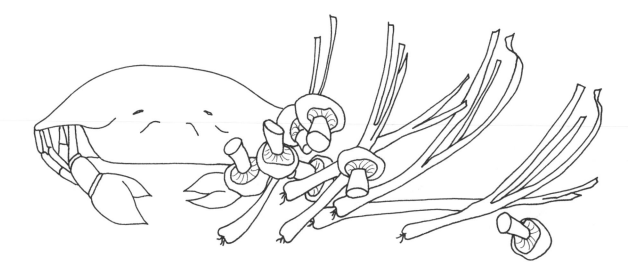

CRAB SPINACH CASSEROLE

Serves 4

    2 eggs, slightly beaten
    1 (10 oz.) pkg. frozen spinach, cooked and well drained
    1/2 tsp. oregano, crushed
    1 (7 1/2 oz.) can cream of mushroom soup
    1/3 Cup celery, large slices
    1/4 Cup sour cream
    2 tsp. flour
    Dash of pepper
    1 (6-8 oz.) pkg. frozen crab (or shrimp), thawed
    1/4 Cup Swiss cheese, grated
    1 Tbsp. butter or margarine, melted
    1/4 Cup bread crumbs, fine

Combine first three ingredients. Spread over bottom and sides of
a greased casserole or individual ramekins. Stir together soup,
celery, sour cream, flour and dash of pepper. Fold in fish and
cheese. Spoon over casserole. Combine crumbs and butter.
Sprinkle on top. Cover and refrigerate overnight.

WHEN READY TO SERVE - Bake uncovered for 30 minutes at 350°.

EGGPLANT STEW

Serves 4-6

    1 1/2-2 Cups onion, sliced
    2 Bell peppers, cored, seeded and chopped
    1 lb. ground beef
    2 Tbsp. oil
    1 small eggplant, peeled if desired and cut into 3/4" cubes
    2 cans (16 oz.) tomatoes
      or 8 fresh tomatoes
    1 pkg. spaghetti sauce mix
    1/4 lb. Mozzarella cheese, sliced
    Croutons

Cook onion, green peppers and beef together in oil until brown and vegetables are tender. Cover eggplant with salt water and then drain. Add to tomatoes, sauce mix and meat mixture. Bring to boil. Cover and simmer for 15 minutes, or until eggplant is tender. Place in a lightly oiled baking dish. Sprinkle with croutons and top with cheese slices. Cover and bake until cheese melts.

WHEN READY TO SERVE - Serve over cooked spinach noodles.

ENCHILADAS - SOUR CREAM AND COTTAGE CHEESE

Serves 6

        1 large can green chilies, cleaned and stripped
        1/4 lb. butter or margarine
        18 corn tortillas
        3 Cups sour cream
        2 Cups farmer style cottage cheese
        Salt and pepper to taste
        1 lb. jack cheese, cut into thin strips

Saute tortillas in butter until softened. Mix together sour
cream, cottage cheese, salt and pepper. Dip tortillas into
mixture and place a chili strip and cheese strip on each tortilla.
Roll up and place in baking dish. Cover with remaining sauce and
bake uncovered for 30 minutes in a 350° oven.

This recipe can be refrigerated overnight and baked the next day.

ENCHILADA CASSEROLE

Serves 6

        1 lb. ground round
        12 corn tortillas
        1 large onion, chopped
        2 (7 oz.) cans green chili salsa
        2 Cups sour cream
        1 Cup cheddar cheese, grated
        2 tsp. salt

Brown meat. Add onion, salt and chili salsa. Simmer 5 minutes.
In a 9" x 13" casserole layer with meat sauce, tortillas, cheese,
sour cream. Repeat 3 times. Cover top with remaining sour cream
and sprinkle with cheese.

Can be made ahead and refrigerated covered overnight.

WHEN READY TO SERVE - Bake covered for 45-50 minutes. Uncover and
cook 5 minutes more.

Freezes well. When thawed, sprinkle with water before baking.

DELUXE ENCHILADA CASSEROLE

Serves 8-10

     1 1/2 lb. ground beef
     1 1/4 oz. pkg. taco seasoning mix
     1 small onion, chopped
     1 Cup water
     1/2 Cup enchilada sauce
     10 corn tortillas
     2 pkgs. frozen chopped spinach, thawed and drained
     3 Cups jack cheese, grated
     1/2 lb. ham, cooked and diced
     1 Cup sour cream

Over high heat, saute beef and onion together, until brown and
meat is crumbly. Add taco seasoning mix and water. Cover and
simmer for 10 minutes.

Lightly coat 5 tortillas in enchilada sauce and overlap them in
the bottom of the baking dish. Add drained spinach to meat
mixture and pour into baking dish. Top with half the cheese.
Repeat with remaining sauce, tortillas and remaining sauce. End
with ham and sour cream on top.

WHEN READY TO SERVE - Bake for 50 minutes in 375° oven. Cover
baking dish for first 25 minutes.

Can be made a day ahead. Cover and refrigerate overnight before
baking.

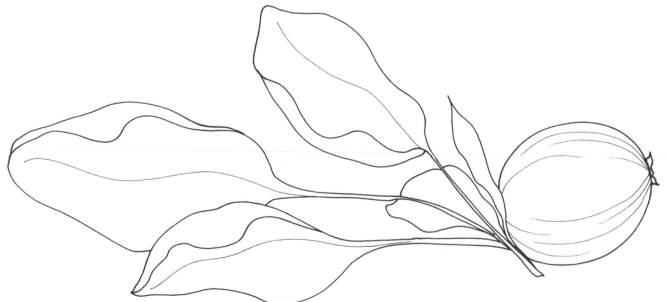

ENCHILADA PIE

Serves 6

    1 1/2 lb. ground round
    1 onion, diced
    1 (16 oz.) can tomatoes
    1 (8 oz.) can tomato sauce
    1 can diced green chilies
    1 pkg. taco seasoning mix
    1 lb. cheddar cheese, grated
    12 corn tortillas
    1 large avocado, sliced

Saute and brown ground round and onion. Add canned tomatoes, tomato sauce and chilies. Add seasoning mix and simmer for 10 minutes.

In an 8 1/2" x 11" baking dish place a layer of tortillas. On top spread a layer of cheese, meat mixture and avocado slices. Repeat tortilla meat mixtures. Cover and refrigerate overnight.

WHEN READY TO SERVE - Bake at 350° for 30-40 minutes until heated through.

EGG AND CHEESE ENCHILADAS

        8 eggs, scrambled
        1 lb. jack cheese, grated
        8 corn tortillas
        2 Tbsp. oil
        1 Lawry's enchilada sauce mix
        1 (6 oz.) can tomato paste
        3 Cups water
        Lettuce, chopped (garnish)
        Tomatoes, chopped (garnish)
        Salsa (garnish)
        avocado, sliced (garnish)
        Sour cream (garnish)

Make enchilada sauce as per directions. Soften tortillas in hot
oil. Drain. Dip tortillas in enchilada sauce. Fill each
tortilla with scrambled eggs and one half of cheese. Roll each
tortilla and place, seam side down in a buttered 12" x 8" x 2"
baking dish. Top with remaining sauce and cheese. Cover and
refrigerate overnight.

WHEN READY TO SERVE - Bake uncovered in a 350° oven for 30-40
minutes. Serve enchilada on a dinner plate and cover with
lettuce, chopped tomatoes and sliced avocados. Top with salsa and
a dollop of sour cream.

This is a meal in itself!

GOULASH

Serves 8

        4 medium onions, chopped
        1/4 Cup oil or shortening
        1 tsp. chili powder
        1 large can tomatoes
        1 lb. spaghetti
        1 1/2 lb. ground round steak
        1 1/2 lb. sausage
        1 can corn
        1 can ripe olives
        1 jar pimentos
        1 can tomato sauce
        1 can tomato soup, optional
        8 oz. cheese, grated

Cook spaghetti until tender, drain and set aside. Saute onions in
oil until tender. Add ground round and sausage and cook until
crumbly. Add chili powder, tomatoes, corn, olives, pimentos,
spaghetti and tomato sauce. Mix well. If more liquid is needed,
add soup.

Place meat mixture in a large flat pan and cover with grated
cheese. Cover and refrigerate overnight.

WHEN READY TO SERVE - Bake at 350° for 45 minutes to 1 hour or
until top is browned.

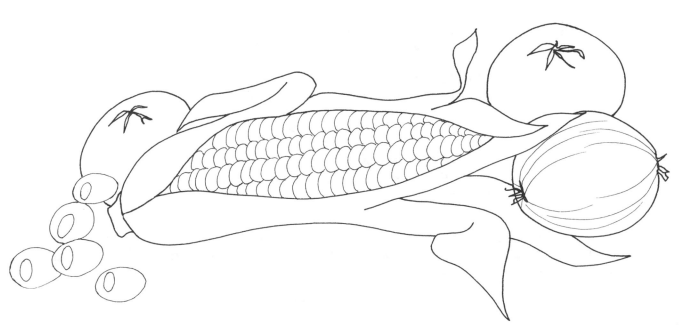

FRANKS AND RICE STRATA

Serves 6

    2 Tbsp. butter
    1 Cup onion, sliced
    2 Cups milk
    1/2 tsp. salt
    1/8 tsp. black pepper
    1/2 tsp. basil
    1/2 Cup flour
    3 Cups rice, cooked
    6 frankfurters, halved
    1 (10 oz.) pkg. frozen chopped broccoli
    6 oz. sharp cheddar cheese, sliced
    Paprika

Sauce onions and butter. Add 1 cup milk, salt, pepper and basil.
Blend remaining milk with flour. Slowly stir into seasoned milk
mixture. Cook, while stirring over medium heat until thick.
Spread rice on bottom of a lightly buttered 11" x 7" casserole.
Layer frankfurters halves and broccoli on top of rice and top with
cheese mixture. Cover with foil and bake at 350° for 25 minutes.

Casserole can be made a day ahead and refrigerated overnight. Add
10 additional minutes for baking when chilled.

HAM LOAF

Grind together: 1 lb. smoked ham
                   2/3 lb. veal

                   1/2 Cup milk
                   4 slices of bread, cut into cubes

                   2-3 Tbsp. onion, minced
                   1/3 Cup celery, finely chopped
                   2-3 Tbsp. vinegar
                   1/4 Cup brown sugar
                   1 egg

Place bread cubes into warm milk. Pour over meat mixture and let
stand until absorbed. Add remaining ingredients and pack into an
oiled loaf pan. Refrigerate overnight.

WHEN READY TO SERVE - Bake uncovered at 350° for one hour.

HAM TETRAZZINI

Serves 6-8

    1 (8 oz.) pkg. thin spaghetti
    1 (6 oz.) jar sliced mushrooms, undrained
    1 small onion, chopped
    1/4 Cup butter or margarine, melted
    1/4 Cup all-purpose flour
    1/2 tsp. dry mustard
    1 1/2 Cups milk
    1 tsp. chicken flavored bouillon granules
    1 tsp. Worcestershire sauce
    2 Cups cooked ham, diced
    1/2 Cup Parmesan cheese, grated

Cook spaghetti according to package, drain and set aside. Reserve liquid from mushrooms and add enough water to mushroom liquid to equal 1 cup, set aside.

Saute onions in butter and cook until tender. While stirring constantly add, flour and mustard. Cook until smooth. Gradually add mushroom liquid, milk, bouillon and Worcestershire sauce.

Cook until mixture thickens and is bubbly. Remove from heat. Excluding cheese, add remaining ingredients and mix well.

Spoon mixture into a greased 2-quart shallow baking dish, cover and refrigerate overnight.

WHEN READY TO SERVE - Bake at 350° covered for 35 minutes. Uncover, sprinkle with cheese and cook for an additional 10 minutes.

HUNGARIAN GOULASH

Serves 5-6

    2 lbs. beef stew meat, cut into 1" cubes
    1 large onion, sliced
    1 clove garlic, crushed
    1/2 Cup ketchup
    1 Tbsp. Worcestershire sauce
    1 Tbsp. brown sugar
    2 tsp. salt
    2 tsp. paprika
    1/2 tsp. dry mustard
    1 Cup water
    1/4 Cup flour

Place meat in a slow-cooking pot. Cover with onions. Combine
seasonings in water and pour over meat. Cover and cook for 9 to
10 hours.

Make a flour paste with a little water and add to meat mixture.
Over high heat stir in paste. Stir until dissolved and cook for
10 to 15 minutes until slightly thickened.

Best made a day ahead and served over noodles or rice.

MONTEREY JACK RATATOUILLE

Serves 6-8

    1 eggplant (about 1/4 lb.)
    1/2 lb. zucchini
    1 green pepper
    7 slices bacon
    1 Cup onion, sliced
    1/8 Cup olive oil
    1/2 Cup tomato paste
    1 1/4 tsp. salt
    1 tsp. garlic, minced
    3 Tbsp. flour
    1 (14 oz.) can sliced tomatoes
    1 (12 oz.) pkg. jack cheese, sliced

Peel and slice eggplant, zucchini and green pepper. Cut bacon
into 2" lengths. Fry bacon with onion stirring often until
cooked. Add olive oil, tomato paste, salt, herbs, garlic, flour
and undrained tomatoes in greased casserole. Layer 1/3 tomato
mixture, 1/3 sliced vegetables and 1/3 cheese. Repeat layers
twice. Bake covered in 400° oven for 50 minutes. Cool,
refrigerate and reheat next day.

INDIAN CURRY CHICKEN
                                                          Serves 4-6

    1 large frying chicken
    2 1/2 Cups milk
    1/2 Cup coconut, grated
    6 strips bacon
    1 large onion, grated
    2 inches of fresh ginger or candied ginger root
    Dash of garlic salt
    4-6 Tbsp. curry powder
    Milk from 1 fresh coconut
    1 Tbsp. flour
    A few drops of almond extract
    Salt, pepper and cayenne to taste

Cook chicken in 1 quart of water. Remove bones and dice meat.
Save the broth and cook down to 1/2 the volume. Scald milk, add
coconut and let stand for 2 hours. Cook the bacon. Saute onion
in bacon fat until golden brown. Add garlic, coconut and coconut
milk. Make a paste of flour and water and add other ingredients.
Cook until thickens. Season to taste and simmer very gently for
20 minutes. Sauce should then be strained or place in blender.
This makes it richer. Add the chicken and if necessary, thin with
the chicken broth. Refrigerate overnight and warm before serving.
Serve with rice.

Condiments to serve with curry: Crumbled bacon, sliced olives,
cubes of glazed bananas and grated coconut. Chopped hard cooked
eggs and green onions. Peanuts and raisins.

This recipe can also be made with 1 1/2 cups cooked lamb, diced.

KOREAN SHORT RIB BARBEQUE

    4 lbs. short ribs, well trimmed and bones sawed through
      (Short ribs to be cut approximately in 2 1/2 pieces)
    1/2 Cup soy sauce
    1/2 Cup water
    1 Cup green onions including tops, chopped
    2 Tbsp. sesame seed
    2 Tbsp. sugar
    2 cloves garlic, crushed
    1/2 tsp. pepper
    1/4 tsp. MSG

Place short ribs into a bowl. Combine remaining ingredients, mix
well and pour over short ribs. Cover and chill overnight in
refrigerator.

WHEN COOKING ON THE BARBEQUE GRILL - Have a hot fire placing ribs
bone side down. When browned turn and cook on meat side. Allow
approximately 15 minutes, exposing all sides to hot surface.
Cook until crispy brown and done to your preference.

Serve with rice and pineapple and other fresh fruits.

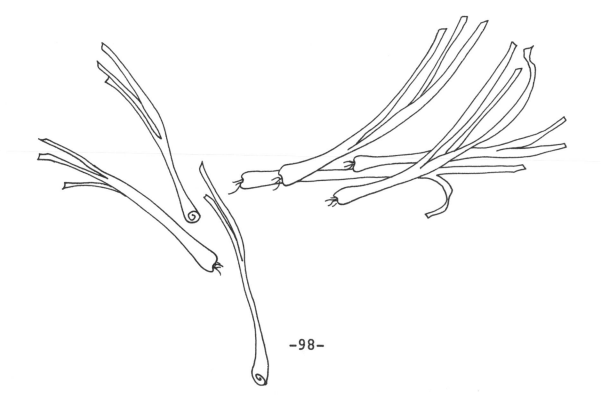

HERBED LAMB AND VEGETABLE KABOBS

Serves 6-8

2 lb. boneless lamb, cut into 1" cubes
1 onion, cut into wedges, blanched
1 green pepper, cut into wedges, blanched
1 red pepper, cut into wedges, blanched

MARINADE:

1/2 Cup cooking oil
1/2 Cup onion, chopped
1/4 Cup parsley, snipped
1/4 Cup lemon juice
1 tsp. marjoram, crushed
1 tsp. thyme, crushed
1 clove garlic, minced
1/2 tsp. pepper

Combine the marinade ingredients in a large bowl and add meat.
Cover and refrigerate overnight.

WHEN READY TO SERVE - Thread skewers, alternating blanched
vegetables and meat. Reserve marinade. Grill on barbecue for 10
minutes, while turning occasionally and brushing with reserved
marinade.

LASAGNA
                                                          Serves 12

Brown together:

    2 Cups ground round
    1 lb. Italian sweet sausage
    1 Cup onion, chopped

Mix together and simmer for 1/2 hour:

    1 (48 oz.) can tomato juice
    1 1/2 lb. fresh mushrooms, sliced
    1 tsp. parsley, minced
    1/2 tsp. salt
    1 (6 oz.) can tomato paste
    1 Tbsp. Worcestershire sauce
    2 tsp. oregano, crushed
    4 cloves garlic, crushed
    1 1/2 tsp. garlic juice

    1 (8 oz.) pkg. long noodles, uncooked
    1 lb. Ricotta cheese, grated
    2 1/2 Cups Mozzarella cheese, grated
    1 1/2 Cup Parmesan cheese, grated

Combine meat and sauce together. In a large lasagna pan pour 5
cups of meat mixture in the bottom. Arrange on top of meat sauce
mixture one half of the uncooked noodles. Again, top noodles with
one half of the meat mixture. By layering, add one half of the
Ricotta cheese, one half of the mozzarella cheese and one half of
the Parmesan cheese. Repeat until reaching the top and ending
with meat sauce mixture. Sprinkle with Parmesan cheese. Cover
and refrigerate overnight.

WHEN READY TO SERVE - Bake uncovered for 45-50 minutes in 350°
oven or until bubbly. Serve with garlic bread and tossed salad.

LASAGNA ROLL UPS
                                              Serves 4-6

        1/2 - (16 oz.) pkg. noodles
        1 Tbsp. salad oil
        1 (10 oz.) pkg. frozen chopped broccoli, thawed and dry
        2 Tbsp. green onion, minced
        2 Cups Ricotta cheese (15 oz.)
        1/4 Cup Parmesan cheese, grated
        1/2 tsp. salt
        1 Cup (4 oz. pkg.) Mozzarella cheese
        1 (21 oz.) jar spaghetti sauce
        1 egg, beaten

Cook noodles according to package, drain and set aside. Saute
onions and broccoli in oil for 5 minutes. Remove from heat. Add
Parmesan and Ricotta cheeses, salt and egg. Set aside.

On waxed paper, place spread out, open noodles. Spread each
noodle with cheese mixture and roll up individually, like a jelly
roll. Place each filled noodle in a lightly oiled 8" x 12" baking
dish, side by side with seam side down. Top with Mozzarella
cheese and remaining sauce.

Before baking cover loosely with foil. Bake for 35 to 45 minutes
or until hot and bubbly. This recipe only makes nine roll-ups.

OLD FASHIONED MACARONI AND CHEESE

Serves 4-6

        1/2 lb. macaroni
        1 tsp. butter
        1 egg, beaten
        1 tsp. salt
        1 tsp. hot water
        1 tsp. dry mustard
        3 Cups sharp American cheese, grated
        1 Cup milk

Cook macaroni according to package, drain. Add butter and egg to macaroni. Mix together mustard, salt and water. Add with milk to macaroni mixture. Before adding cheese, reserve 1/2 cup for topping. Pour into a buttered casserole and top with cheese. Cover and refrigerate overnight. Before baking allow to stand for 20 minutes.

WHEN READY TO SERVE - Bake at 350° for 45 minutes or until custard is set and top is crusty.

MEAT AND MACARONI CASSEROLE

Serves 6

        1 3/4 Cups uncooked macaroni
        2 Cups pork, beef, ham, lunch meat, chicken or turkey,
          finely chopped
        2 Cups milk
        1/2 lb. American cheese, grated
        2 cans cream of mushroom soup
        4 hard cooked eggs, diced (garnish)
        Parsley and pimento, chopped (garnish)

With the exception of garnishes combine all ingredients and mix well. Place in 3-quart greased baking dish, cover and refrigerate overnight.

WHEN READY TO SERVE - Bake covered at 350° for 1 1/4 hours. Garnish with egg, parsley and pimento. Serve immediately.

MACARONI AND SPINACH CASSEROLE

Serves 10-12

    5 cans macaroni and cheese
    2 pkgs. frozen chopped spinach, thawed and squeezed dry
    1 small bunch green onions, finely chopped
    1/2 tsp. oregano
    1/4 lb. cheese, grated (garnish)
    1 can French fried onion rings (garnish)

Excluding garnishes mix together and pour into baking dish. Top with grated cheese and onion rings, cover and refrigerate overnight.

WHEN READY TO SERVE - Bake @ 350° for 3/4 to 1 hour. Serve immediately.

MEXICAN BEEF WITH ORANGE

Serves 6

              3 lbs. round steak
              1 Bay leaf
              1 onion, chopped
              1/2 Cup water

PASTE: 2 cloves garlic, crushed
              1/2 tsp. ground cloves
              1 tsp. coriander
              Salt and pepper to taste

              2 cups orange juice
              1 orange, sliced (garnish)

Make paste of garlic, cloves, coriander, salt and pepper. Make cuts in round steak and fill with some paste in each cut.

Place meat in heavy skillet with water, Bay leaf and onion. Simmer until tender. Remove from heat, cool and cut into thin slices. Cover with orange juice and chill overnight covered, turning occasionally.

WHEN READY TO SERVE - Garnish with orange slices and serve cold.

PASTITSA

Serves 20-24

    3 lbs. macaroni
    1 1/2 lb. ground pork
    1 1/2 lb. ground lamb
    Fresh mint, chopped
    1 large onion, sliced thin
    1/2 tsp. butter
    Parmesan cheese
    Salt and pepper to taste

    TOPPING:

    6 eggs, beaten
    1 quart half and half

Cook macaroni according to package. Drain. DO NOT RINSE. Set
aside. Mix together, pork, lamb and mint. Set aside.

In a buttered roasting pan place macaroni. Sprinkle with Parmesan
cheese. Layer with meat, macaroni and cheese. Layer to top,
ending with cheese.

Mix together eggs and half and half. Pour mixture over top of
meat mixture. Cover and refrigerate overnight. Before serving
let stand at room temperature for 20 minutes.

WHEN READY TO SERVE - Bake at 350° for 45 minutes.

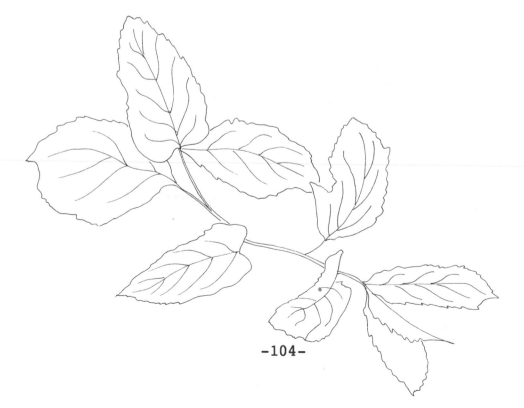

PORK CHOP CASSEROLE

Serves 4

        4 pork chops
        1 can cream of mushroom soup
        2 Cups rice, cooked and drained
        2 Tbsp. green pepper, chopped
        2 Tbsp. pimentos
        2 Tbsp. green onions, chopped

Brown pork chops and set aside. Butter a baking dish. Mix
together, rice, peppers, onions and pimentos. Place rice mixture
in bottom of dish. Top with pork chops. Pour cream of mushroom
soup over top. Cover and refrigerate overnight.

WHEN READY TO SERVE - Bake covered in 350° oven for 45-50 minutes.

RED FLANNEL HASH

        1 1/2 Cups cooked meat, chopped,
          turkey, ham, beef or corned beef
        2 Cups potatoes, boiled and cubed
        1 Cup beets, boiled and cubed
        3 Tbsp. onion, finely chopped
        1/2 Cup light cream
        Salt and pepper to taste

Lightly mix all ingredients together and place in buttered
casserole. Refrigerate overnight.

WHEN READY TO SERVE - Bake at 325° for 1 hour, until crusty on
top.

SAILORS STEW

Serves 6

    3 Tbsp. butter or margarine
    1 medium onion, sliced
    2 lbs. round steak, cut into 1/2" cubes
    2 Cups potato, thinly sliced
    1 (12 oz.) can of beer
    1 tsp. salt
    1/2 tsp. pepper
    1/2 tsp. thyme

Saute onions until lightly brown in butter. Remove from pan.
Pound meat into 1/2" strips. In the same skillet saute meat until
brown. Alternate layers of meat, onion and potato in a 2-quart
buttered casserole. In the same meat skillet pour in beer, add
seasonings and stir until hot. Pour over casserole. Cover and
refrigerate overnight. Before baking, let stand at room
temperature for 20 minutes.

WHEN READY TO SERVE - Bake covered for 1 hour at 350°.

MAKE-AHEAD SAUSAGE SOUFFLE

Serves 4

    1/4 lb. hot bulk pork sausage
    4 eggs, beaten
    3 slices white bread, crumbled
    1 1/2 Cups milk
    1 tsp. salt
    1 tsp. dry mustard
    1 Cup cheddar cheese, grated

Brown sausage, stirring until crumbly. Drain off fat, reserve and
set aside. Beat eggs until light in color. Add bread crumbs,
milk, salt, mustard and sausage to beaten eggs. Fold in cheese.
Spoon into 1-quart souffle dish. Cover and refrigerate overnight.

WHEN READY TO SERVE - Bake for 1 hour at 325° or until knife
inserted into center comes out clean. Serve immediately.

SHEPHERD'S PIE

Serves 4

    2 Tbsp. butter or margarine
    2 Tbsp. flour
    1/2 tsp. salt
    Dash of thyme and pepper
    1/2 Cup water
    1 tsp. instant bouillon
    1/3 Cup sauterne or white table wine
    1 Tbsp. instant minced onion or 1/2 Cup onion, finely chopped
    2 Cups cooked lamb, diced
    1/2 Cup celery, thinly sliced
    1 (3 3/4 oz.) pkg. instant mashed potatoes
    1 Tbsp. butter or margarine (garnish)

Melt butter and blend in flour, salt, thyme and pepper. Gradually
stir in water. Add instant bouillon, wine and onion. Stir until
mixture thickens and boils. Add lamb and celery. Turn into
shallow greased baking dish, cover and refrigerate overnight.

WHEN READY TO SERVE - Make mashed potatoes according to package
and smooth over top. Dot with butter. Bake in very hot oven
(450°) for about 20 minutes, until lightly browned on top. Serve
at once from baking dish.

ITALIAN SPAGHETTI AND MEAT BALLS

Serves 6

1 1/2 lb. ground beef

MEAT MIXTURE:

1/2 Cup fine dry bread crumbs
1 egg, slightly beaten
1/4 Cup Parmesan cheese, grated
1/4 Cup warm water
1 1/2 tsp. salt
1/2 tsp. basil
1/4 tsp. pepper

SAUCE MIXTURE:

1 (6 oz.) can tomato paste
1/4 Cup onions, chopped
2 cloves garlic, crushed
2 Tbsp. parsley, chopped
1 Tbsp. salt
1 tsp. oregano
1/4 tsp. anise seed
1 (#2 1/2) can (3 1/2) Cups tomatoes

1 lb. long spaghetti

Add ingredients of meat mixture to ground beef and mix well. Form
36 - 1" balls. Brown slowly in hot oil. Add sauce ingredients to
skillet and simmer uncovered. DO NOT BOIL. Stir occasionally for
the next 1 1/2 to 2 hours or until thickened. Cover and
refrigerate overnight.

WHEN READY TO SERVE - Cook spaghetti according to package, drain
and serve with heated meat balls and sauce.

SPAGHETTI PIE

Serves 4-6

    6 oz. spaghetti, broken in half
    2 eggs, beaten
    1/4 Cup Parmesan cheese, finely grated
    2 Tbsp. butter
    1/3 Cup onion, chopped
    1 Cup sour cream
    1 lb. Italian sausage, remove casing
    1 (6 oz.) can tomato paste
    1 Cup water
    4 oz. Mozzarella cheese, sliced

Cook spaghetti in boiling salted water until tender. Drain and
add eggs and Parmesan cheese. Pour into a well greased 10" pie
pan, making sure spaghetti covers well. Melt butter, add onion
and saute until limp. Add sour cream and spoon over spaghetti.
Cook sausage until browned and crumbly. Drain. Mix with tomato
paste and water, and spoon on top of sour cream mixture. Cover and
refrigerate overnight.

WHEN READY TO SERVE - Remove from refrigerator and let stand at
room temperature for 20 minutes. Bake uncovered at 350° for 35
minutes. Top pie with cheese and return to oven for about 10
minutes, until cheese melts.

This freezes well, so make two at a time and freeze one for later.

SHRIMP ASPARAGUS CASSEROLE

        2 lbs. shrimp, (fresh or frozen) clean and deveined
        2 tsp. salt
        1 quart water
        2 (15 oz.) cans long green asparagus spears, drained
        2 (1 1/4 oz.) pkgs. hollandaise sauce mix
        4 hard cooked eggs, sliced
        1 1/2 Cups milk
        2 Tbsp. cooking oil
        1/2 Cup sour cream
        1 Tbsp. margarine or butter, melted
        3/4 Cup dry bread crumbs
        1 Tbsp. Parmesan cheese, grated

Boil shrimp 30 seconds in boiling water. Rinse shrimp under cold
water until cool. Drain and set aside. Arrange asparagus spears
in bottom of a well greased approximate 12" x 8" x 2" baking dish.
Place shrimp evenly over asparagus, layer egg on top.

Combine hollandaise sauce mix with milk and cooking oil over low
heat, stirring constantly. Stir until thickened. Remove from heat
and stir in sour cream. Spoon hollandaise mixture evenly over
shrimp and eggs. Combine margarine, bread crumbs and cheese and
spread on top. Cover tightly and refrigerate overnight.

WHEN READY TO SERVE - Bake uncovered in moderate oven, 350° for 30
minutes or until thoroughly heated.

SHRIMP SOUFFLE
                                                        Serves 4-6

        4 cans shrimp
          or 2 (8-10 oz.) frozen pkgs. shrimp
        6 eggs
        4 Cups milk
        12 slices white bread, crusts off
        2 Cups sharp cheddar cheese, grated
          mustard
        Salt and pepper to taste

Spread bread with butter and mustard. Place six slices in bottom
of buttered 8" x 13 1/2" baking dish. Cover bread with shrimp and
cheese. Place remaining bread slices on top. Beat egg yolks into
milk and set aside. Beat egg whites until stiff and fold into egg
yolk milk mixture. Pour on top of casserole. Cover and
refrigerate overnight.

WHEN READY TO SERVE - Bake for 1 hour and 20 minutes in 325° oven.

TALLARINA

Serves 10

    1 large onion, chopped
    1 green pepper, cut fine
    1 clove garlic, crushed
    1 Tbsp. vegetable oil
    1 large can tomatoes
    1 large package wide noodles
    1 1/2 - 2 lbs. ground round
    1 can Mexican or plain corn
    1 can ripe olives
    1 can stuffed olives
    1 can sliced or whole mushrooms
    1 can enchilada sauce

Saute onion, green pepper and garlic in oil. Add tomatoes and
simmer for 10 minutes. Prepare noodles according to package,
drain and add to vegetables. Saute meat until crumbly. Drain and
add to noodle mixture. Add remaining ingredients. Mix well.
Place in a casserole and add cheese on top. Cover and refrigerate
overnight.

WHEN READY TO SERVE - Bake for 45 minutes in 350° oven.

TAMALE PIE

Serves 6-8

    1 can tomatoes
    1 lb. ground round
    2 onions, chopped
    1 can corn
    1 can black olives
    3/4 Cups corn meal
    Salt and pepper to taste

Saute ground round until crumbly. Drain off fat. Add chopped
onions, tomatoes, corn and olives. Stir well. Slowly add corn
meal while stirring. Add salt and pepper to taste. Place
ingredients in buttered casserole, cover and refrigerate
overnight.

WHEN READY TO SERVE - Bake for 1 hour at 350°.

EASY TAMALE PIE

Serves 6

    2 tamales (from deli), cut up
    1 lb. ground round steak
    1 large onion, minced
    1 (#2) can creamed corn
    1 (8 oz.) can tomato sauce
    1 can tomato soup
    1 tsp. garlic powder
    1 tsp. chili powder
    1 tsp. salt
    1 Cup cheddar cheese, grated
    Fresh parsley or cilantro (garnish)

Brown meat and onions together. Add remaining ingredients
excluding cheese. Put in a baking dish and top with cheese.
Refrigerate overnight.

WHEN READY TO SERVE - Bake uncovered in 350° oven for 40-50
minutes. Serve hot.

TORTILLA CASSEROLE

1 lb. ground beef
1 onion, chopped
1 clove garlic, minced
1 can (4 1/2 oz.) chopped ripe olives
1 can (8 oz.) tomato sauce
6 corn tortillas, cut into bite size pieces
1/2 lb. (2 Cups) sharp cheddar cheese, grated
1/2 tsp. salt
1/4 tsp. pepper
1 Tbsp. chili powder
1 lb. can barbecued beans (optional)
  or 1 lb. can chili beans (optional)

Saute meat until crumbly. Drain. Add onion and garlic. Add seasonings, olives and tomato sauce. Simmer 10 minutes. In a 2-quart casserole alternate layers of tortillas, meat sauce and cheese, ending with cheese on top. Cover and refrigerate overnight.

WHEN READY TO SERVE - Bake for 30-40 minutes covered in 350° oven.

TANGY TUNA CASSEROLE

Serves 4

        1/4 Cup green pepper, chopped
        3 Tbsp. butter or margarine, melted
        2 Tbsp. flour
        1 Cup milk
        1/2 small onion, grated
        2 tsp. prepared mustard
        1 tsp. prepared horseradish (optional)
        1 tsp. lemon juice
        Salt and pepper to taste
        1 (7 oz.) can tuna, drained and flaked
        2 hard-cooked eggs, sliced
        1 (17 oz.) can whole kernel corn, drained
        1 Cup (4 oz.) cheddar cheese, grated

Saute green pepper in butter over low heat. Cook until tender.
Add flour, stirring until smooth. Cook for 1 minute, stirring
constantly. Gradually add milk. Cook over medium heat, stirring
constantly until thickened and bubbly. Add onion, mustard,
horseradish, lemon juice, salt and pepper.

Grease a 1-quart casserole. Spoon in one half of corn, eggs,
tuna, sauce mixture and half of the cheese. Repeat layers until
filled. Cover and refrigerate overnight.

WHEN READY TO SERVE - Let stand at room temperature for 20
minutes. Bake uncovered for 30 minutes at 350°. Sprinkle with
remaining cheese and bake for an additional 5 minutes or until
cheese melts.

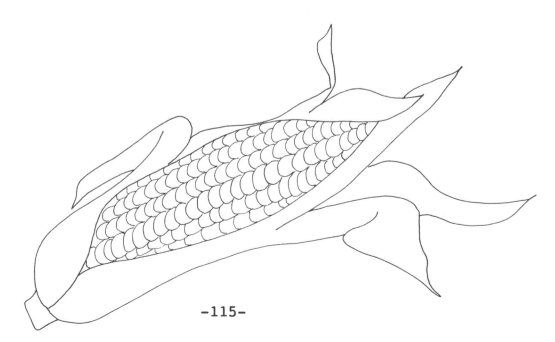

CURRIED TURKEY

Serve 4

        1 Cup turkey, cooked and cubed
        1 Cup sour cream
        1/2 tsp. curry powder
        1/4 Cup onion, chopped
        1 Tbsp. butter
        1 can cream of mushroom soup
        1/4 Cup milk
        Parsley, snipped (garnish)
        1 Cup rice

Saute onions in butter for 10 minutes. Stir in soup and milk.
Stir until smooth. Add sour cream and curry powder. Stir until
smooth. Add turkey. Cover and refrigerate overnight.

WHEN READY TO SERVE - Prepare rice according to directions, drain
and set aside. Heat turkey mixture until hot. Serve over
prepared rice and garnish with parsley.

Yummy dish when you have left over turkey.

ZUCCHINI ENCHILADAS

Serves 6-12

        1 large onion, chopped
        1/2 cube butter or margarine.
        4-5 zucchini, sliced and cut into quarters, blanched
        1/2 lb. jack cheese, grated
        1 pint sour cream
        12 flour tortillas
        1 pkg. enchilada sauce
        1/2 lb. cheddar cheese, grated

Saute onion in butter until tender. Add blanched zucchini. Add
jack cheese and sour cream. Mix well. Remove from heat. Soften
tortillas in oil and lay out flat. Prepare enchilada sauce
according to package directions and set aside. Fill each tortilla
with zucchini mixture and roll up. Place in well oiled casserole,
side by side, seam side down. Pour over enchilada sauce and top
with cheddar cheese. Can be refrigerated, covered overnight.

WHEN READY TO SERVE - Bake for 30-40 minutes at 350° until hot and
bubbly.

Holiday
Treats

ALMOND COOKIES

                                            Makes 4 dozen

Mix together: 2 Cups butter or margarine
                2 Cups sugar
                1 can almond paste

Next add
and mix: 2 eggs

Then add: 1 1/2 tsp. salt
                1 1/2 tsp. soda
                5 Cups flour
                1 Cup almonds, chopped

Dip: 1 (12 oz.) pkg. chocolate chips
                1 tsp. milk

Mix everything together and add 1 cup chopped almonds. Roll into
1 1/2" logs and roll in chopped almonds. Bake @ 350° for 10
minutes.

Melt 1 (12 oz.) package chocolate chips with 1 tsp. milk. When
cookies are cool, dip each end into chocolate mixture. Store in
a tightly covered container and serve or give as gifts.

ALMOND CHRISTMAS COOKIES

                                            Makes 2 dozen

                1 Cup butter
                1 Cup sugar
                1 Cup ground almonds (unblanched)
                2 Cups flour
                1/2 tsp. salt
                1 tsp. vanilla

Mix all ingredients together and pat thickly (1/8") on a floured
board. Cut into cookies with a small cutter.

Bake @ 350° for 15 minutes and while still warm, roll in
granulated sugar.

These are delicious and will keep all during the holidays, if kept
in a covered container.

ALMOND LACEY COOKIES

Makes 7 dozen

           2/3 Cups grated almonds (3 1/4 oz. package)
           1/2 Cup butter
           1/2 Cup sugar
           2 Tbsp. each milk and flour

Combine all ingredients. Heat until butter melts. For each
cookie, spoon 1/2 tsp. warm batter onto a baking sheet covered
with foil - - space 2 1/2" apart.

Bake @ 350° for 6-7 minutes. Let cool about 10 minutes on cookie
sheet. Then transfer to wire rack to cool completely.

These are very fancy and nice for a Christmas cookie plate.

ALMOND SQUARES

Makes 2 dozen

               1 Cup almonds
               1 egg white, unbeaten

Cream
together: 1/4 lb. butter
               1/2 Cup sugar

Then add: 1 egg yolk (save egg white)
               1 Cup flour
               1/4 tsp. cinnamon

Cream butter and sugar. Add remaining ingredients. Spread on a
cookie sheet, so as to have the dough about 1/8" thick. Blanch
almonds and place an inch apart on cookie dough. Glaze with
unbeaten egg white. Bake for 1 hour @ 250°. Cut in squares and
store in covered container.

This is a family recipe that we use every Christmas for serving
or giving as gifts.

BANANA BREAD

Makes 1 large loaf

          1/2 Cup butter or margarine
          1 Cup sugar
          2 eggs
          3 mashed ripe bananas
          2 Cups flour
          1 tsp. soda
          1/2 Cup chopped nuts
          Pinch of salt
          1 tsp. vanilla

Cream butter and sugar. Add slightly beaten eggs and bananas.
Mix dry ingredients and add nuts and vanilla.

Bake in a greased loaf pan @ 350° for 40 minutes - 1 hour.

This is better made ahead and wrapped in foil or plastic bag. It
freezes nicely.

CHRISTMAS CAKE (JOLAKAKA)

Makes 2 loaves

          1/2 Cup shortening
          1 1/2 Cups sugar
          3 eggs
          3 Cups flour
          3 tsp. baking powder
          1/2 tsp. salt
          1/4 tsp. cardamom
          1 Cup raisins
          1/2 Cup citron, chopped
          1 Cup milk

Cream shortening, sugar and eggs together. Sift flour, baking
powder and salt. Add alternately with milk to the creamed
mixture. Add cardamom, raisins and citron. Bake in a greased
loaf pan in a 350° oven for 1 hour.

BUTTERBALLS

Makes 4 dozen

> 1 pound butter
> 1 cup powdered sugar
> 4 1/2 Cups flour
> 2 tsp. vanilla
> 2 Cups chopped nuts

Mix all ingredients together and form into balls (about the size of a walnut).

Bake on an ungreased cookie sheet @ 300° for 45 minutes. Roll twice in powdered sugar and store in a covered container.

Make these cookies ahead to serve at Christmas or give as gifts.

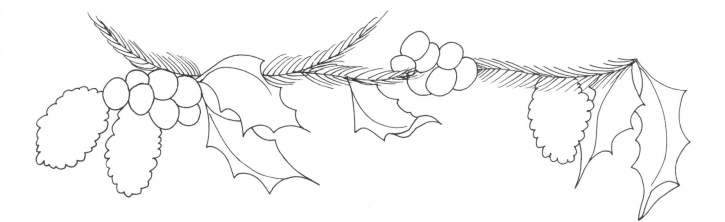

CHRISTMAS NUTS

> 1 pound shelled pecan halves
> 1 Cup brown sugar
> 3 1/2 Tbsp. canned milk (regular)

Boil brown sugar and canned milk for 3 minutes and let stand for 10 minutes. Beat again for 2-3 minutes. Mix with pecans. Separate and cool on waxed paper.

These are delicious to serve, or to put in containers and give as gifts.

CRANBERRY BREAD

Makes 1 loaf

2 Cups flour
1/2 Cup sugar
1 Tbsp. baking powder
1/2 tsp. salt
2/3 Cup fresh orange juice
2 eggs, beaten slightly
3 Tbsp. sweet butter, melted
1/2 Cup coarsely chopped nuts
1 1/2 Cups cranberries
2 tsp. grated orange rind

Preheat oven to 350°. Grease loaf pan.

Sift flour, sugar, baking powder and salt into a mixing bowl.
Make a well in the middle of the sifted mixture and pour in orange
juice, eggs and melted butter. Mix well, but don't over mix.
Fold in nuts, cranberries and orange rind.

Pour batter in pan and rest on middle rack of oven. Bake 45-50
minutes @ 350° or until knife inserted comes out clean. Cool in
pan for 10 minutes...remove from pan and cool completely on rack.

Wrap in foil or put in plastic bag for 1-2 days before serving.

This bread is an especially nice gift during the holidays.

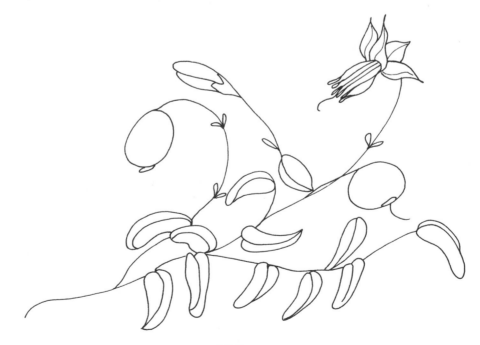

DATE AND NUT SQUARES

Makes 16 - 2" squares

Beat until foamy:

2 eggs

Beat in:

1/2 Cup sugar
1/2 tsp. vanilla

Sift together and stir in:

1/2 Cup sifted flour
1/2 tsp. baking powder
1/2 tsp. salt

Mix in:

1 Cup chopped walnuts
2 Cups finely chopped dates

Spread in well greased 8" square pan. Bake until top has a dull crust (325° for 25-30 minutes). Cut into squares while warm...cool and remove from pan. If you desire, dip in powdered sugar.

Store in covered container...will keep very well.

LINZERTART

Makes 4 dozen

Mix: 1/2 lb. margarine
                1 Cup sugar

Add: 3 egg yolks

Mix well and
gradually add: 3 Cups flour

Dough will be soft. Press dough onto buttered 10" x 15" jelly
roll pan with your fingers. Do not take dough to edge of pan.
Bake @ 350° for 15 minutes or until light brown. Cool 5 minutes.
Spread with raspberry jam, sprinkle with 1 Cup chopped pecans.
Cut in squares while warm. Remove from pan when cool.

These store well in covered container.

SAND KAGE (DANISH CAKE)

                1 lb. butter
                2 Cups sugar
                4 Cups flour
                8 eggs
                2 Tbsp. cocoa

Cream butter and sugar. Add eggs and flour. Beat until well
mixed. Divide batter in half and add cocoa to one half of the
batter.

In a greased loaf pan, put plain half of the batter and top with
chocolate batter. Bake in a 350° oven for 1 hour.

This stores well to serve as a holiday dessert. Also, nice to
give as a gift.

CHRISTMAS PERSIMMON PUDDING

Cream:

1 Cup sugar
1 Tbsp. melted butter

Add:

1/2 Cup milk (mixed with 2 tsps. soda)
Pulp of 2 persimmons, chopped
1 Cup flour
1 1/2 tsp. baking powder
Pinch of salt

Mix well and pour into oiled mold and steam for 2 hours.

This will store in refrigerator or freezer.

SERVE WITH THIS SAUCE:

Cream together:

1 Cup sugar (granulated)
2 Tbsp. melted butter

Add:

1 egg yolk, beaten (save white)

Fold in:

1 egg white, stiffly beaten
1/2 pint whipped cream
1 tsp. vanilla

Sauce can be made ahead. It keeps nicely in refrigerator for at least a week.

This is our family traditional Christmas dessert.

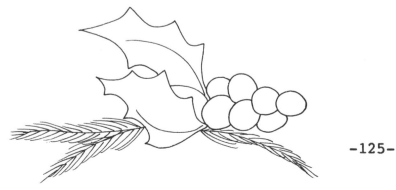

ROSETTES (Danish Christmas cookie)

Mix in order:

2 eggs, well beaten
1/4 tsp. salt
1 Tbsp. sugar
1 Cup flour
1 Cup milk

Dip hot Rosette iron in batter and fry in deep fat until crisp.
Drain shells on paper towels.

Sprinkle with powdered sugar.

These Rosettes store well in covered containers and are "A Must"
to serve at Christmas time.

SAND BAR KELSE (butter cookie)

1 Cup butter or margarine
1 Cup sugar
Pinch of salt
1 egg or 2 egg yolks
1/2 tsp. vanilla
1/2 tsp. almond extract
2 Cups flour

Mix all ingredients together,
Roll in 1" balls and dip in sugar. Press down with glass and
bake on ungreased cookie sheet. Bake in oven @ 350° for 10 - 12
minutes.

These cookies keep well in covered container.

SANTA COOKIES

Makes 5-6 dozen

Cream:

1 Cup shortening
4 Cups brown sugar

Add and mix:

4 eggs, well beaten
6 Cups flour (mixed with 1 Tbsp. soda)
1 tsp. vanilla

The dough will be stiff. Roll dough into logs, cover with plastic wrap and refrigerate overnight.

Slice and bake on greased cookie sheet in 350° oven for 10 minutes.
Frost each cookie with thin frosting.

FROSTING: 1 lb. box powdered sugar
                1/2 cube soft butter
                1 Cup warm milk
                1 tsp. vanilla

Add a little more warm milk if frosting isn't thick enough.

Decorate with holly and red hots. Store in covered container.

Our children always left a plate of these cookies for Santa on Christmas Eve.

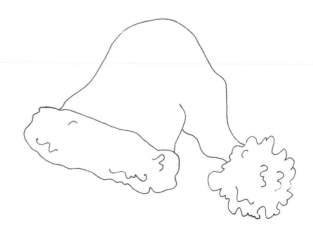

Party
Appetizers

ARTICHOKE AND EGG PATE

Serves 20-30

    1 (16 oz.) can artichoke hearts, chopped
    6 hard boiled eggs
    1 Cup sour cream
    1 Cup mayonnaise
    Salt and pepper, to taste
    1/4 tsp. curry powder or dry mustard
    Parsley or pimentos

Mix together - artichoke hearts and eggs in food processor until
coarsely chopped - add - sour cream, mayonnaise, salt & pepper and
curry powder (or mustard) - blend - until smooth. Pour into
lightly oiled mold and refrigerate overnight.

WHEN READY TO SERVE - Remove from mold, garnish with parsley or
pimentos and serve with crackers or melba toast.

ARTICHOKE CANAPE

Serves 20-30

    2 jars marinated artichoke hearts, drained
    1 bunch green onions
      or 1 onion, chopped fine
    1 clove garlic, minced
      or 1 tsp. garlic powder
    4 eggs, beaten with fork
    1 tsp. salt
    1/8 tsp. each - curry, oregano, pepper and
      Worcestershire sauce
    2 Cups cheddar cheese, grated
    1/4 Cup parsley, minced

Chop artichokes finely and save liquid.

Saute onion & garlic for 5 minutes in a small amount of artichoke
oil. Add remaining ingredients (except parsley) and pour mixture
into 8" x 8" pan and refrigerate over night.

Bake @ 325° for 30 minutes.

WHEN READY TO SERVE - Cut into tiny squares, garnish with minced
parsley and serve warm.

BROCCOLI DIP

Serves 10-12

    1 (10 oz.) pkg. frozen chopped broccoli
    2 hard cooked eggs, chopped
    1 Cup mayonnaise
    3 Tbsp. grated Parmesan cheese
    1 Tbsp. fresh lemon juice
    1 Tbsp. prepared mustard
    1/2 tsp. salt
    Pepper to taste
    Paprika garnish

Cook the broccoli according to package directions. Drain and press out liquid. Drop broccoli into food processor, using steel blade, and process until fairly fine. Add remaining ingredients and mix well.

Chill in refrigerator overnight to allow flavors to blend.

WHEN READY TO SERVE - Sprinkle paprika over top. Use as a dip with cut vegetables or spread very thinly on crackers.

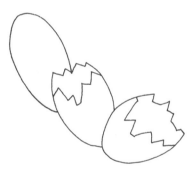

HOT CANAPES

Serves 10

    1 can ripe olives, chopped
    3/4 Cups mayonnaise
    1/2 cup Parmesan cheese
    2 Tbsp. green onion, chopped
    Curry powder to taste
    1 loaf French bread or buffet rye

Mix ingredients together, cover and refrigerate overnight.

WHEN READY TO SERVE - Spread thinly on sliced French bread or buffet rye and place under broiler for approximately 4-5 minutes or until melted and lightly browned. Serve warm.

CHEESE APPETIZER

Serves 12

          1/2 pound sharp cheddar cheese, grated
          1/2 pound margarine (at room temperature)
          1/2 tsp. Tabasco sauce
          1/2 tsp. Worcestershire sauce
          1 tsp. salt
          2 Cups flour
          2 Cups Rice Krispies (rolled with rolling pin)

Mix by hand - cheese and margarine. Add seasonings. Blend in
flour and Rice Krispies. Roll into 1" balls, flatten with fork.
Refrigerate overnight.

WHEN READY TO SERVE - Bake for 18 minutes @ 325°. Serve warm. A
great hot hors d'oeuvre.

CHILI CHEESE SQUARES

Serves 20-30

          1 (7 oz.) can diced green chilies, drained
          12 oz. shredded sharp cheddar cheese
          1 (4 oz.) can diced pimentos, drained
          4 eggs, separated
          2 Tbsp. flour
          1 tsp. salt
          10 stuffed olives, sliced
          Fresh cilantro, chopped (garnish)

Place chilies in bottom of greased 9" square baking dish - layer -
pimentos and olives. Beat egg whites until stiff, but not dry.
Fold in lightly beaten egg yolks, flour and salt. Spread over
layered ingredients and sprinkle with grated cheese.

Bake @ 350° for 30 minutes. Cool. Store in refrigerator
overnight. Re-heat when ready to serve.

WHEN READY TO SERVE - Cut into tiny squares and serve warm.
Garnish with chopped cilantro.

CHEESE BALL #1

Serves 20

                4 (8 oz.) pkgs. cream cheese
                1/4 Tbsp. Tabasco
                1 Tbsp. Worcestershire sauce
                1/2 pound bleu cheese
                1 small jar sharp cheese
                1 clove garlic, minced
                1 Cup minced parsley (divide in one half)
                1 Cup pecans, finely chopped (divide in one half)

Let cheeses stand until room temperature. Mix all ingredients
together - except - 1/2 Cup pecans and 1/2 Cup parsley. (Save for
garnish.) Shape into ball and chill overnight.

To garnish roll ball onto remaining parsley and pecans. Wrap in
plastic wrap and refrigerate until hardened and ready to serve.

WHEN READY TO SERVE - Serve with assorted crackers.

CHEESE BALL #2

Serves 20

                6 oz. of bleu cheese
                2 (5 oz.) jars cheddar cheese
                4 (3 oz.) pkgs. cream cheese
                1 tsp. Worcestershire sauce
                1/2 tsp. Accent
                2 Tbsp. grated onion
                1 Cup chopped pecans (divide in one half)
                1/2 Cup minced parsley (divided in one half)

Let cheeses stand until room temperature. Mix all ingredients
together - except - 1/2 Cup pecans and 1/4 Cup parsley. (Save for
garnish.) Shape into ball and chill overnight.

To garnish - roll ball onto remaining parsley and pecans. Wrap in
plastic wrap and refrigerate overnight or hardened and ready to
serve.

WHEN READY TO SERVE - Serve with assorted crackers.

CHIPPED BEEF DIP

Serves 12

        1 (8 oz.) pkg. cream cheese
        2 Tbsp. milk
        1 (2 1/2 - 3 oz.) jar chipped beef, finely chopped
        1 Tbsp. onion, minced
        2 Tbsp. green pepper, diced
        1/4 tsp. seasoned pepper
        1/2 tsp. sour cream
        1/4 tsp. sliced almonds
        Parsley (garnish)

Blend together and refrigerate overnight.

When served hot- Heat in an un-greased casserole dish for 15-20 minutes @ 350°.

WHEN READY TO SERVE - Garnish with parsley sprig and serve with crisp crackers.

Can be served hot or cold.

OLIVE CHEESE BALLS

Serves 20

        2 Cups cheddar cheese, grated finely
        1 Cup flour
        4 Tbsp. soft butter
        Dash of pepper
        1 or 2 jars stuffed green olives

Mix all ingredients together - except - olives. Roll mixture around each stuffed olive and place on waxed paper. Cover and refrigerate overnight.

WHEN READY TO SERVE - Bake on an un-greased cookie sheet @ 375° for 15-20 minutes or until lightly browned. Place colorful tooth pick in each one and serve hot.

MEXICAN CHEESE SPREAD

Serves 8

        1 (8 oz.) pkg. cream cheese, softened
        1 medium avocado, mashed
        1 green onion, finely chopped
        1 clove garlic, minced
        1 tsp. fresh lemon juice
        1 (7 oz.) can chopped green chilies, drained
        Cilantro (garnish)

Mix together all ingredients and blend well. Cover tightly and
chill in refrigerator overnight, so flavors will blend.

WHEN READY TO SERVE - Garnish with cilantro and serve with
crackers or tortilla chips.

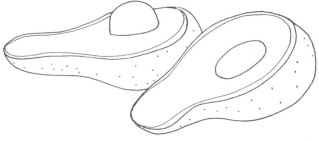

PINEAPPLE CHEESE BALL

Serves 20

        2 (8 oz.) pkg. cream cheese, softened
        1 (8 1/2 oz.) can crushed pineapple, well drained
        2 Cups walnuts, chopped (divide in one half)
        1/4 Cup green pepper, finely chopped
        2 Tbsp. onion, finely chopped
        1 Tbsp. seasoned salt
        Grapes (for garnish)

In a bowl thoroughly mix cream cheese until smooth. Gradually add
pineapple, green pepper, onion, salt and one half of the walnuts,
(save 1 cup for garnish).

Shape mixture into a ball. Roll in remaining nuts and wrap in
plastic wrap. Refrigerate overnight.

WHEN READY TO SERVE - Garnish with grapes and serve with a variety
of crackers.

BAKED CHICKEN WINGS

Serves 12

        3 pounds chicken wings (split chicken wings)
        1 Cup soy sauce
        1/2 Cup brown sugar
        1 Cup honey
        1 tsp. dry mustard
        1/2 Cup white wine
        1 Tbsp. vinegar
        3/4 Tbsp. cinnamon
        1/2 tsp. ground ginger

In a plastic bag - mix marinade ingredients together. Add chicken to mixture in bag and let stand overnight in refrigerator.

Bake @ 400° in a 10" x 13" pan for 1 hour. Cover with foil for first half an hour. Remove foil and continue cooking for 20 - 30 minutes.

Serve warm.

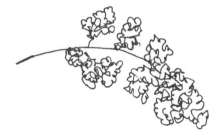

CRAB MEAT PUFFS

Serves 6-8

        1 can crab meat (or rock lobster)
        1/2 cup sharp cheddar cheese, grated
        1/2 cup mayonnaise
        2 Tbsp. grated onion
        1/4 Cup parsley, minced (for garnish)
        Paprika (garnish)
        1 small box of melba toast rounds

Mix all ingredients together (except parsley). Cover and refrigerate overnight.

Bring mixture to room temperature before spreading on melba rounds. Place under broiler 4-5 minutes or until puffy and lightly browned.

WHEN READY TO SERVE - Garnish with parsley and a dash of paprika. Serve hot.

COMPANY CRAB MOUSSE

Serves 12

1 can cream of mushroom soup
1 (8 oz.) pkg. cream cheese, softened
1 envelope unflavored gelatin
1 (6 1/2 oz.) can crab meat, rinse and drain
1/2 Cup cooked shrimp, cut into small pieces
1 Cup celery, diced
1/2 Cup green onion, chopped
1 Tbsp. fresh lemon juice
1 tsp. Worcestershire sauce
1/4 tsp. seasoned salt
Light cooking oil
Parsley (garnish)

Lightly oil a 4 Cup mold.   In a saucepan, over low heat, combine
soup, cream cheese and gelatin - stir until smooth and creamy
(about 1-2 minutes).   Remove from heat - add remaining
ingredients.   Pour mixture into prepared mold.   Cover and chill in
refrigerator overnight.

Delicious ... Remove from mold on to serving dish.   Garnish with
parsley and serve with assorted crackers.

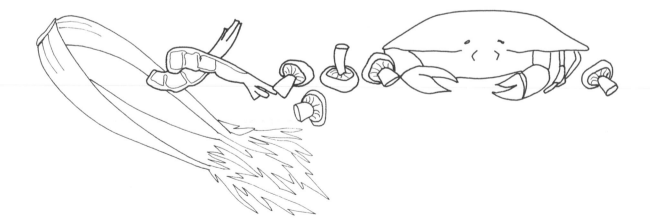

DILL DIP

Serves 6-8

> 1 (3 oz.) pkg. cream cheese, softened
> 1/2 tsp. grated lemon rind
> 1 1/4 Tbsp. fresh lemon juice
> 1/4 tsp. dill weed
> 1/8 tsp. salt
> 1 Tbsp. onion flakes
> 1 Tbsp. parsley flakes
> 1 tsp. Beau Monde seasoning salt
> 2/3 Cups sour cream
> 2/3 Cups mayonnaise
> Paprika (garnish)

Combine all ingredients - except - sour cream and mayonnaise. Beat until fluffy, blend in sour cream and mayonnaise. Chill overnight in refrigerator.

WHEN READY TO SERVE - Sprinkle paprika over top and serve as dip with crackers.

EMPANADAS

> 1 Cup butter, softened
> 1 (8 oz.) pkg. cream cheese
> 2 Cups flour
> 1 pound lean ground beef
> 1 pkg. spaghetti sauce mix or taco mix
> 1 tsp. seasoned salt
> 1/2 cup water
> 2 medium tomatoes, peeled and chopped
> 1/4 Cup onion, finely chopped
> 1/2 Cup cheddar cheese, grated
> 2 Tbsp. Parmesan cheese
> Paprika
> 1 bunch cilantro, minced

For dough mixture - cream butter and cream cheese until well blended. Add flour and combine thoroughly. Refrigerate while making filling.

Brown ground beef until crumbly. Add spaghetti sauce or taco mix, seasoned salt, water, tomatoes and onion to meat. Stir often while simmering for 15 minutes. Remove from heat, add cheeses and combine thoroughly. Let cool.

Roll dough out to about 1/8" thickness. Cut dough with a 3" round cutter. Place 1 tsp. of meat mixture onto 1/2 of each dough circle. Wet edges, fold over and crimp edges with fork. Place Empanadas on cookie sheet and freeze. After frozen, place in plastic bag and keep in freezer until ready to bake.

WHEN READY TO SERVE - bake @ 350° for 15-20 minutes or until brown. Sprinkle with minced cilantro and serve warm as a hot hors d'oeuvre.

These are a favorite at every party.

JALAPENO JELLY DIP

6-8 sm. jars

1/2 Cup fresh lemon juice
1 Cup white vinegar
2 Cups green bell pepper, cored and seeded
1/2 cup yellow hot chili peppers
    or 1 can Jalapenos
1/4 medium onion
4 1/2 Cups sugar
1 (6 oz.) bottle of Certo
8 drops green food coloring
1 pkg. cream cheese

Remove stems, seeds and rinse Jalapenos before placing in blender
with lemon juice, vinegar, green peppers and onion. Mix at high
speed until well blended. Remove from blender and add sugar.
Boil mixture rapidly for 5 minutes in a large pot. Remove from
stove and add Certo. Cook for 2 more minutes. Skim off foam and
add green food coloring.

Pour into sterile glass jars and seal immediately with paraffin.
Let cool and refrigerate overnight.

WHEN READY TO SERVE - Spread over cream cheese and serve with
crackers.

Jars of Jalapeno jelly make nice holiday gifts.

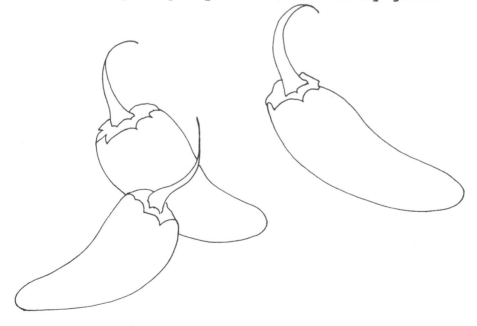

MARINATED MUSHROOMS

Makes 6 small jars

         2 pounds button mushrooms
         1/4 Cup fresh lemon juice
         1 Tbsp. minced parsley
         2 Tbsp. minced onion
         2 Tbsp. chopped pimento
         1 clove garlic, minced
         1/2 tsp. sugar
         1/2 tsp. salt
         1/8 tsp. oregano
         1/8 tsp. pepper
         1/4 Cup water
         1/4 Cup olive oil
         1/2 Cup cider vinegar

Wipe any dirt from mushrooms and trim stems. Place mushrooms
in a large sauce pan and cover with water. Add lemon juice and
bring to boil - simmer for 1 minute. Drain.

Combine mushrooms with remaining ingredients. Pack in sterilized
jars and seal. Store in refrigerator at least 24 hrs. or longer.

WHEN READY TO SERVE - Drain off liquid and serve with toothpicks.
Serve on tray with assorted blanched vegetables.

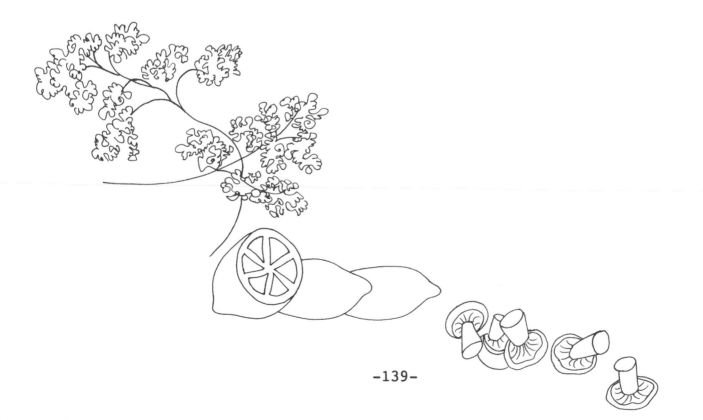

ONION PARTY PUFFS

Makes 40 puffs

      1 (8 oz.) pkg. of refrigerator biscuits
      1/3 Cup onion soup mix
      1/2 pound butter or margarine
      Parsley, minced (for garnish)

Soften butter or margarine and mix with onion soup mix. Makes
1 1/4 cups.

Cut each biscuit into 4 sections. Dot with onion butter. Place
on un-greased shallow baking pan. Cover and refrigerate
overnight.

WHEN READY TO SERVE - Preheat oven to 400° and bake for 8 minutes
or until golden brown. Garnish with parsley and serve hot on
serving tray.

PARTY SALSA

Serves 10-12

      2 cans tomatoes, drained and chopped
      2 can diced green chilies, drained
      2 cans diced pimentos, drained
      2 cans diced olives, drained
      1 onion, chopped
      1/2 pound jack cheese, grated

Mix together and chill in refrigerator overnight.

WHEN READY TO SERVE - Serve with tortilla chips or as a side dish
with a Mexican dinner.

PIMENTO STUFFED SNOW PEAS

Serves 12

              1/2 pound fresh snow peas
              1 pkg. pimento cream cheese

Bring 3/4 Cup of water to boil. Place peas into water and cook
for 1-2 minutes. Rinse in cold water until cold to touch and
drain.

Split seams of snow peas and fill with pimento cream cheese.
Cover and chill overnight in refrigerator.

WHEN READY TO SERVE - Serve as an appetizer or as a salad. They
are really colorful and delicious!

SALMON BALL

Serves 25

              1 (8 oz.) pkg. cream cheese, softened
              1 Tbsp. fresh lemon juice
              1 pound can of salmon
              1/4 Cup onion, grated
              1/2 tsp. prepared horseradish
              1/2 Cup pecans, chopped
              1/2 Cup parsley, minced

Remove all skin from salmon. Mix together with ingredients
except - pecans and parsley (use for garnish) and form into
ball. Cover and place in refrigerator over night. Day of
serving, roll ball in pecans and parsley.

WHEN READY TO SERVE - Serve with a variety of crackers.

SHRIMP DIP

Serves 6-8

        1 can cream of shrimp soup
        1 (8 oz.) pkg. cream cheese
        1 Tbsp. chopped stuffed olives
          (save out 1 whole olive for garnish)
        1 tsp. Worcestershire sauce
        Dash of garlic salt
        Dash of Tabasco
        Paprika (garnish)

Mix in food processor until smooth.   Cover and chill in
refrigerator overnight.

WHEN READY TO SERVE - Garnish with whole olive on top and a
sprinkle of paprika. Serve with a variety of crackers.

MARINATED SHRIMP

Serves 8

        1 pound fresh mushrooms, cleaned and quartered
        1 Cup water
        1/3 Cup Spanish olive oil
        2/3 cup vinegar
        2 Tbsp. fresh lemon juice
        2 cloves garlic, halved
        1 1/4 tsp. salt
        1/2 tsp. thyme leaves
        1/2 tsp. peppercorns
        1/8 tsp. nutmeg
        2 bay leaves
        3/4 Cup pimento stuffed olives
        2 pounds medium shrimp, cleaned and cooked

Combine all ingredients - except olives and shrimp -in 1 Cup
water. Cover, bring to boil and cook for 5 minutes. Remove from
stove, pour into bowl, add olives and shrimp. Cool. Cover and
refrigerate overnight.

WHEN READY TO SERVE - Drain and serve over crushed ice with
toothpicks.

SHRIMP MOLD

Serves 20-30

                2 (5 oz.) cans shrimp, drained (save juice)
                  (hold out 7 shrimp for garnish)
                2 eggs, hard cooked and chopped finely
                1 cup mayonnaise
                2 Tbsp. capers
                2 pkgs. plain gelatin
                1 fresh lemon, squeezed
                1 Tbsp. onion juice
                2 shakes of Tabasco sauce
                Parsley sprigs (garnish)

Soften gelatin in 2 Tbsp. water. Dissolve softened gelatin
in 1 cup warm water and juice of 1 lemon. Flake canned
shrimp. Add remaining ingredients and pour in greased mold.

Cover and store in refrigerator overnight.

WHEN READY TO SERVE - Serve on colorful plate and garnish with
seven shrimp and parsley sprigs. Serve with a variety of
crackers.

SHRIMP STARTER

Serves 8-10

                2 beef bouillon cubes
                  or 2 tsp. instant beef bouillon
                1 Tbsp. hot water
                1 (8 oz.) pkg. cream cheese
                1 tsp. sour cream
                2/3 Cups finely chopped celery
                2-4 green onions, finely chopped
                1 (4 1/2 oz.) can tiny shrimp, drained
                Parsley sprig (garnish)

Dissolve bouillon in hot water. Beat in cream cheese and sour
cream until smooth. Add remaining ingredients and stir well.
Cover and store in refrigerator overnight.

WHEN READY TO SERVE - Garnish with sprig of parsley and serve with
raw cut vegetables and/or a variety of crackers.

SPINACH DIP

                                                    Serves 8-10

        2 (10 oz.) pkgs. frozen chopped spinach, drained
        1 Cup sour cream
        1/2 Cup mayonnaise or salad dressing
        1/2 parsley, minced
        1/2 onion, minced
        1 tsp. salt
        1/2 tsp. celery salt
        1/4 tsp. pepper
        1/8 tsp. nutmeg
        Cherry tomatoes or pimento slices (garnish)

Squeeze raw spinach dry, add remaining ingredients. Mix well,
cover and store in refrigerator overnight.

WHEN READY TO SERVE - Garnish with pimento slices or halved cherry
tomatoes and serve with a variety of cut raw vegetables.

QUICK SPINACH DIP

                                                    Serves 8-10

        1 Cup mayonnaise
        1 Cup sour cream
        1 can water chestnuts, drained and chopped
        1 pkg. frozen chopped spinach, drained
        1 pkg. vegetable soup mix
        Pimento or paprika (garnish)

Squeeze spinach dry, mix with remaining ingredients. Cover and
store in refrigerator overnight.

WHEN READY TO SERVE - Sprinkle paprika over top, or garnish with
slice of pimento. Serve with raw cut vegetables or a variety
of crackers.

SPINACH BALLS

Makes 60 balls

2 (10 oz.) pkgs. frozen chopped spinach
1 (6 oz.) pkg. chicken-flavored stuffing
1 Cup Parmesan cheese, grated
6 eggs, lightly beaten
3/4 Cup butter or margarine, melted
salt & pepper to taste

Cook spinach according to package directions. Drain well by
pressing out all excess liquid.

Combine all ingredients and mix well. Roll into balls (1 1/2")
the size of large marbles. Place on a cookie sheet and freeze.
When frozen store in plastic bags in freezer.

WHEN READY TO SERVE - Replace frozen balls on cookie sheet and
bake @ 350° for 10-15 minutes or until lightly browned. Serve
hot.

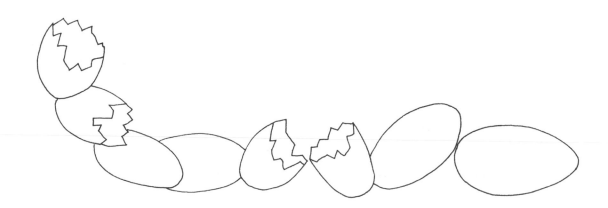

STAR BRIGHT ASPIC

> 1/2 Cup pimento stuffed olives, sliced
> 1/4 Cup sharp cheese, grated
> 2 pkgs. lemon Jell-O
>   (Dissolve Jell-O in 1 Cup boiling water)
> 2 - (12 oz) cans V8 juice
> 1 Tbsp. vinegar
> 1 Tbsp. Worcestershire
> Few dashes of Tabasco
> Coarse ground pepper
> 1 lb. cooked baby shrimp (garnish)
> 2 hard boiled eggs (garnish)
> Parsley sprigs (garnish)

Mix together and pour into a round tube mold that has been greased with mayonnaise.

Sauce: 1 Cup mayonnaise
                1/2 Cup ketchup
                1 Tbsp. lemon juice

Mix together.

WHEN READY TO SERVE - Unmold and fill center of mold with cooked baby shrimp. Garnish with sliced eggs and parsley sprigs. Top with sauce.

This is a very nice dish to serve before a Christmas dinner or at a party buffet.

CHERRY TOMATO APPETIZER

Serves 12

        2 boxes cherry tomatoes
        1/2 white onion, finely diced
        1/2 cucumber, diced
        1/2 green pepper, finely diced
        1/4 Cup mayonnaise
        1 Tbsp. fresh lemon juice
        1/8 tsp. dill weed
        Salt & pepper to taste
        Dash of Worcestershire sauce
        Parsley (garnish)

Cut tomatoes in half. Scoop out 1/2 of pulp in each half and place in bowl. Trim off bottoms of tomatoes, so they will sit straight and store prepared shells upside down on dish in refrigerator (covered) until ready for filling.

Add all ingredients (except parsley) to removed tomato pulp and toss lightly. Cover and chill in refrigerator until ready to fill tomatoes.

WHEN READY TO SERVE - Fill each tomato with just enough mixture to softly mound on top and at the same time, easily pop into your mouth. Garnish with parsley and serve cold.

SHRIMP BUTTER

        8 oz. shrimp, cooked and chopped
        8 oz. cream cheese, softened
        1/4 Cup butter, softened
        2 Tbsp. scallions, minced (whites only)
        4 Tbsp. lemon juice
        1/4 tsp. dried dill weed
        2-4 drops Tabasco sauce
        1/4 tsp. salt
        White or rye, sliced thin

Excluding bread, mix ingredients together. Place in a crock, cover and refrigerate overnight.

WHEN READY TO SERVE - Serve on thinly sliced bread.

LAYERED TOSTADA SPREAD

Serves 12-16

    1 can refried beans
    1 Cup guacamole dip
    2 to 3 green onions, chopped
    1 Cup sour cream
    1 small can chopped black olives
    2 tomatoes, chopped
    1 (7 oz.) can diced green chilies
    1 Cup cheddar cheese, grated

Layer in serving pan, starting with beans and ending with cheese.
Cover and refrigerate overnight.

WHEN READY TO SERVE - Serve with large tortilla chips.

It's a party favorite.

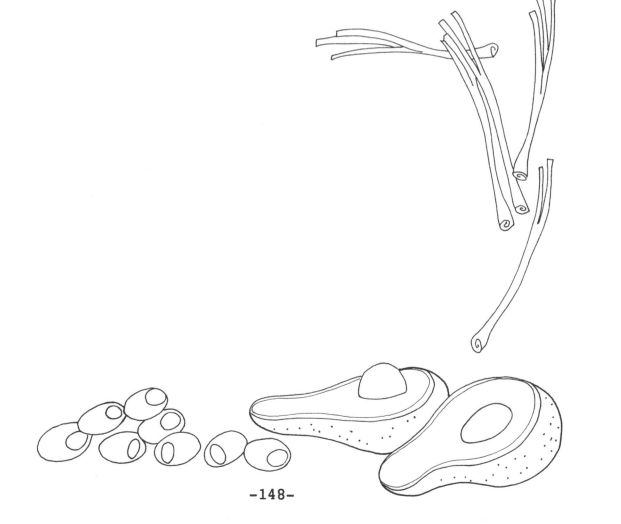

Salads

APPLE CRUNCH SALAD

Serves 9

              1 (6 oz.) strawberry Jell-O
              1 3/4 Cups boiling water
              1 1/2 Cups apple juice
              1/4 tsp. cinnamon
              1 Cup apples, peeled and finely chopped
              1/2 Cup celery, diced finely
              1/4 Cup pecans, chopped

Dissolve Jell-O in boiling water. Stir in apple juice and
cinnamon. Chill until consistency of unbeaten egg white. Stir in
remaining ingredients. Pour into oiled 8" square Pyrex pan.
Chill overnight.

24-HOUR SALAD

Serves 12

              2 eggs, beaten
              3 Tbsp. vinegar
              3 Tbsp. sugar
              2 Tbsp. butter
              1 Cup whipped cream
              2 cans white cherries
              2 cans pineapple chunks
              2 oranges, seeded and chopped
              2 cups marshmallows, cut into quarters

Put eggs in double boiler over boiling water. Add vinegar and
sugar. Beat constantly until thick and smooth. Remove from heat
and add butter. When cool, fold in whipped cream and fruit and
marshmallow mixture. Turn into lightly oiled ring mold and
refrigerate overnight.

WHEN READY TO SERVE - Unmold on serving plate.

It is a nice luncheon salad.

8 BEAN SALAD

                                                    Serves 35

                    1 (1 lb.) can lima beans
                    1 (1 lb.) can butter beans
                    1 (1 lb.) can kidney beans
                    1 (1 lb.) can red beans
                    1 (1 lb.) can whole green beans
                    1 (1 lb.) can cut green beans
                    1 (1 lb.) can pinto beans
                    1 (1 lb.) can wax beans
                    1/2 Cup green pepper, chopped
                    1 Cup red onion, chopped
                    1 Cup vinegar
                    1 1/2 Cups oil
                    2 Tbsp. sugar, salt and pepper to taste

Drain beans and mix with green pepper and onion in a large bowl.
Mix vinegar, oil, sugar, salt and pepper and pour over beans.
Allow to marinate overnight. Drain off dressing before serving.
Dressing can be stored in covered jar in refrigerator and used
again.

DISGUISED BOLOGNA

                                                    Serves 6

                    1/2-1 lb. bologna, remove skin
                        and cut thinly into shoestring strips
                    1 can consomme (the kind that jells)
                    3/4 cup mayonnaise
                    1 head lettuce (garnish)
                    Olives and radishes (garnish)

Mix together consomme and mayonnaise. Add bologna strips and
cover. Refrigerate overnight.

WHEN READY TO SERVE - Serve on lettuce and garnish with olives and
radishes. Good as a summer lunch salad.

BAKED BEAN SALAD

Serves 6

        1 (20 oz.) can baked beans, thoroughly drained
        1/2 Cup mayonnaise
        1/4 Cup celery, diced
        1/4 Cup onion, grated
        1/4 Cup green pepper, chopped
        1/4 Cup dill pickles, chopped

Mix all together, cover and chill overnight in refrigerator.

Double this recipe and take it to a potluck.

WHEN READY TO SERVE - Serve on a lettuce leaf.

LAYERED BEAN AND BEET SALAD

Serves 8-10

        2 cans sliced pickled beets, drain and quarter
        2 cans dilled green beans, drain
        6 green onions, chopped (tops and all)
        1 Cup Best Foods mayonnaise
        2 Tbsp. sugar
        4 hard cooked eggs, grated (garnish)

Layer: 1 can of drained and quartered beets, one half of green
onions and 1 can drained green beans. Repeat. When completed
sprinkle sugar on top. Cover top with mayonnaise to edge of bowl.
Cover and chill in refrigerator overnight.

WHEN READY TO SERVE - Sprinkle grated hard cooked eggs on top.

PICKLED BEET SALAD

Serves 12-16

        1 (3 oz.) pkg. strawberry Jell-O
        1 (3 oz.) pkg. raspberry Jell-O
        1 (3 oz.) pkg. cherry Jell-O
          Dissolve in 4 Cups boiling water
        1 (#305) can French cut beets,
          drain and save liquid
        1/2 Cup sweet pickle juice
        1 (#303) can crushed pineapple, drained

Add 1 cup combined pineapple and beet juice and 1/2 cup pickle
juice to Jell-O mixture. Chill in refrigerator until syrupy.
Stir in beets and pineapple. Pour into lightly oiled 3-quart mold
or oiled 9"x13"x2" pan,cover and chill overnight in refrigerator.

DRESSING   Mix together:

        1 Cup mayonnaise
        1 Tbsp. green onion, minced
        1 Tbsp. celery, finely chopped
        1 Tbsp. green pepper, finely chopped

This is a favorite salad for Christmas dinner.

BROCCOLI SALAD

Serves 8

        1 1/2 bunches fresh broccoli, chopped finely
        10-12 slices crisp bacon, crumbled
        1 cup red seedless grapes
        1 medium red onion, finely chopped

Mix broccoli and onions together, add grapes and bacon and toss.

DRESSING   1 Cup mayonnaise
                1/4 Cup sugar
                2 Tbsp. vinegar

Pour over salad and stir.

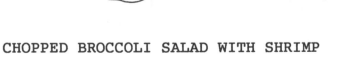

CHOPPED BROCCOLI SALAD WITH SHRIMP

Serves 6

        2 stalks broccoli, finely chopped
        2-3 green onions, finely chopped
        1 can water chestnuts, drained and finely chopped
        1 can tiny shrimp, drained
        1/2 Cup sunflower seeds or slivered almonds
        1/2 cup mayonnaise
        2 Tbsp. vinegar

Mix ingredients together and chill overnight.

BRUSSELS SPROUTS SALAD

Serves 8

    4 Cups brussels sprouts, trimmed and washed
    1 Cup cherry tomatoes, halved
    1 Cup vegetable oil
    1/3 Cup wine vinegar
    1 1/2 tsp. sugar
    1 tsp. salt
    2 Tbsp. green onion, minced
    2 Tbsp. green pepper, minced
    2 Tbsp. parsley, minced
    4 drops Tabasco
    1 head romaine lettuce (garnish)

Halve each brussels sprout lengthwise. Cook covered in boiling water for 15 minutes and drain. In a jar combine remaining ingredients, excluding lettuce and tomatoes, cover tightly and shake well before pouring over brussels sprouts and tomatoes. Cover and chill overnight to season.

WHEN READY TO SERVE - Serve in bowl that has been lined with romain leaves.

TELEPHONE MEMO

COLDWELL BANKER COMMERCIAL

DATE _____

TO _____   TIME _____

CALLER _____

OF _____

PHONE

AREA CODE   NUMBER | EXTENSION

☐ TELEPHONED   ☐ PLEASE CALL

☐ CAME TO SEE YOU   ☐ WILL CALL AGAIN

☐ RETURNED YOUR CALL ☐ WANTS TO SEE YOU

☐ HOLDING ON EXTENSION _____

MESSAGE _____

_____

_____

_____

SIGNED _____

—325— about 1 in

internal 115 f
for hard

— knife & cube server

BLUEBERRY, RASPBERRY JELL-O SALAD

Serves 10-12

        1 large pkg. black raspberry Jell-O
          Dissolve Jell-O in 2 Cups boiling water
        1 can blueberries
        1 small can crushed pineapple
        1/2 - 1 Cup chopped nuts
        1 carton whipped topping

Strain blueberries and pineapple and add enough cold water to make
1 1/2 to 2 cups. Set aside 1/2 cup mixture. Add dissolved Jell-O
and nuts. Let jell and refrigerate overnight. Mix 1/2 cup saved
liquid with whipped topping. At serving time spread over top.

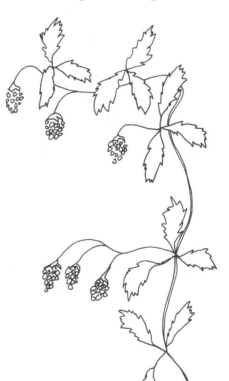

DRY JELL-O SALAD

Serves 20

        1 large whipped topping
        1 pint sour cream
        1 pint cottage cheese
        2 pkgs. any flavor Jell-O, dry
        1 (#2) can crushed pineapple, drained

Mix all ingredients together and chill overnight before serving.

This is easy to make and very tasty.

BULGUR WHEAT SALAD

Serves 6

                1 Cup bulgur wheat
                1/3 Cup green onion, sliced
                1/2 Cup celery, diced finely
                1/3 Cup walnuts, toasted
                1/3 Cup (or more) dates, chopped

Cook bulgur wheat in salted boiling water for 5-10 minutes, until tender. Rinse in cold water. Drain and fluff when cool.

Combine with remaining ingredients and toss with dressing. Cover and refrigerate.

DRESSING   Mix together:

                1/8 tsp. cinnamon
                3 Tbsp. lemon juice
                1/3 Cup olive oil
                Salt and pepper to taste

Best made a day ahead to blend seasonings.

CENTERPIECE SALAD

Serves 25-50

> 8 red potatoes, cooked, peeled and chopped
> 2 hard cooked eggs, chopped
> 1/2 Cup celery, diced
> 2 dill pickles, chopped

Combine ingredients with: 1/2 Cup mayonnaise
                                1 Tbsp. prepared mustard
                                Salt and pepper to taste

Store covered in refrigerator overnight.

> For garnish:
>
> 1 head lettuce
> 6 oz. Muenster or Swiss cheese, sliced
> 6 tomatoes, cut into wedges
> 3 cucumbers, cut into thin strips
> 5 avocados, peeled and cut into thin wedges
>   Cover avocados with juice from 1 lemon
> 2 Cups ham, cubed or cooked shrimp
> 1 (7 1/2 oz.) can pitted ripe olives, drained
> 2 green peppers, cut into rings
> 1 bunch radishes
> 2 Tbsp. oregano, crushed

Line a 14" platter or basket with large lettuce leaves. Mound
potato salad in center. Shred remaining lettuce and place on top
of potato salad. Cover with cheese slices.

Starting at base of salad mound, place alternating rings of tomato
wedges, cucumber sticks and avocado wedges. Attractively place
cubed ham or shrimp between wedges and decorate with pepper rings,
olives and radishes. Sprinkle with crushed oregano. Cover
tightly with plastic wrap and refrigerate overnight.

WHEN READY TO SERVE - Drizzle choice of dressing over salad and
cut into wedges at table, using a pie server.

This is a huge salad and very exciting to serve at a large party.

CHICKEN ALMOND MOUSSE SALAD

Serves 8

    1 pkg. lime gelatin
    1 pkg. unflavored gelatin
      Dissolve gelatin in 1 1/2 Cups boiling water
    1 Cup chicken broth, warm
    3 Cups chicken, cooked and diced
    1/4 Cup celery, diced
    1/2 Cup almonds or water chestnuts, chopped
    1 Cup whipped cream
    2 Tbsp. parsley, chopped
    1/2 Cup cucumber, chopped
    1 Tbsp. lemon juice
    2 tsp. salt
    1 Cup cottage cheese (garnish)
    Olives and parsley sprigs, (garnish)

Mix gelatins and water together, until dissolved. Add chicken broth and set aside. Add chicken, celery, almonds, cucumbers, parsley, lemon juice and salt. Chill until thickened. Fold in whipped cream and pour into an oiled mold and chill overnight.

WHEN READY TO SERVE - Unmold onto serving plate, spread cottage cheese on top and garnish with olives and parsley sprigs.

Great for "luncheon" to serve with spiced peaches, pineapple and banana bread or date-nut bread.

CHICKEN PASTA SALAD

Serves 12

3 Cups white chicken meat, cooked and chopped
1 lb. mixed colored pasta, cooked and drained
1 Cup green seedless grapes
1 small can mandarin oranges, drained
1 med. can pineapple chunks, drained & cut fine
1/2 Cup almonds, slivered or sliced
1 bell pepper, chopped
2 raw carrots, chopped
2 stalks celery, diced
Add to 1 (8 oz.) bottle coleslaw dressing,
1/2 Cup mayonnaise and 1 tsp. curry powder

Mix all ingredients together and chill overnight in a covered bowl in refrigerator.

I served this at a bridal shower and it was a big success.

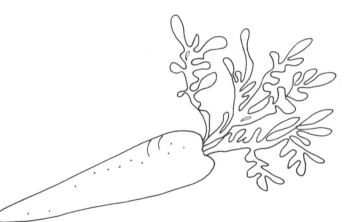

CHICKEN AND POTATO SALAD

Serves 12

12 cooked potatoes, cut into small pieces
2 boiled chickens, cut meat into small pieces
3 hard boiled eggs, chopped
1 quart Best Foods mayonnaise
1 large onion, chopped
1/4 Cup parsley, minced
Salt and pepper to taste

Combine all ingredients and mix well. Refrigerate overnight for flavors to mix well.

This is great for a dinner salad served with a vegetable or fruit and rolls.

CHICKEN STACK-UP SALAD
Make 24 hours ahead

Serves 8

          2 Cups cooked chicken, diced
          1/4 tsp. salt
          1/4 tsp. paprika
          1/8 tsp. lemon-pepper seasoning

Toss first four ingredients together and set aside.

          4 Cups lettuce, shredded
          1 Cup celery, diced
          1 (10 oz.) frozen English peas, thawed
          1 1/2 Cups elbow macaroni, cooked
          1 Cup mayonnaise
          1 (8 oz.) carton sour cream
          1/2 lb. cheddar cheese, grated (garnish)

Layer lettuce, chicken mixture, celery, peas, cheese and macaroni
in that order in a 4 quart bowl. Combine mayonnaise and sour
cream and mix well. Spread mixture evenly over the top of the
salad to the edge of bowl. Cover tightly and chill overnight.

WHEN READY TO SERVE - Top with cheese.

CHINESE VEGETABLE SALAD

             1 can fancy mixed vegetables, drain
             1 can chop suey vegetables, drain
             1 can petite young peas
             1/2 Cup salad oil
             1/2 Cup vinegar
             3/4 Cup granulated sugar
             1/2 tsp. salt
             1/2 tsp. pepper

Place drained vegetables in glass bowl. Mix together oil and
vinegar with sugar, salt and pepper. Pour over vegetables and
cover to marinate overnight.

WHEN READY TO SERVE: Pour off any extra liquid before serving.

This liquid can be refrigerated and used again as a salad dressing
or as a marinade.

LAYERED COLESLAW

Serves 12

        1 head green cabbage, thinly shredded
        2 sweet white onions, peeled and thinly sliced
        1/4 Cup sugar
        1 tsp. prepared mustard
        1/2 tsp. dry mustard
        1 Cup cider vinegar
        Salt and pepper to taste
        1 tsp. celery or caraway seed
        3/4 Cup salad oil

Prepare cabbage and separate onions into rings. In a bowl layer
cabbage, onion rings and sugar. Combine remaining ingredients in
saucepan and heat to boil. Remove from heat and pour over cabbage
layer. Cover and refrigerate overnight.

WHEN READY TO SERVE - Toss slaw and add more salt if desired.

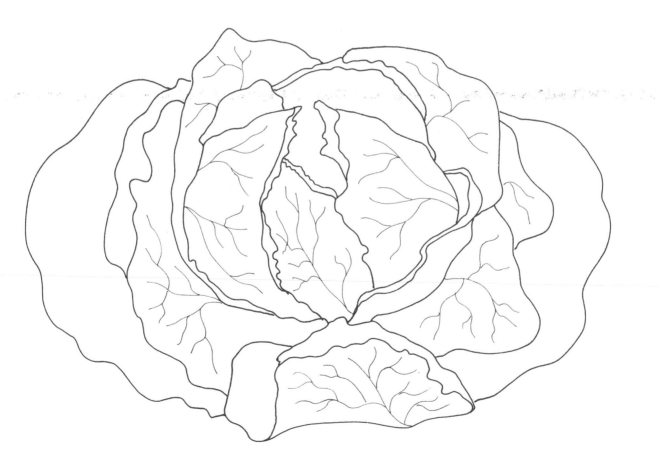

CRAB-SHRIMP SALAD

                                                           Serves 8

                    1 loaf white sandwich bread,
                      crusts removed and cut into pieces
                    3 Cups mayonnaise
                    4 hard boiled eggs, chopped
                    2 cans crabmeat, drained
                    2 cans shrimp, drained
                    1/2 Cup onions, chopped
                    1 Cup celery, diced
                    1 tiny jar pimento
                    Salt and pepper
                    Lettuce leaves (garnish)
                    Olives (garnish)
                    Relish (garnish)

Mix all ingredients together, cover and chill in refrigerator
overnight.

WHEN READY TO SERVE - Spoon onto lettuce leaf and garnish with
olives and relish.

FROZEN CRANBERRY SLICES
Make the day before

                                                           Serves 8-9

                    1 (#2) can crushed pineapple, drained
                    1 can cranberry sauce (whole berry)
                    1/2 pint sour cream
                    1/4 Cup pecans, chopped
                    Lettuce greens

The day before combine all ingredients except greens. Turn into
freezing tray and mold, refrigerate overnight.

WHEN READY TO SERVE - Cut into slices and serve on crisp salad
greens.

CRANBERRY AND GRAPE SALAD

Serves 8-10

        1 lb. raw ground cranberries
        1 Cup sugar
        1 lb. seedless grapes, halved
        1 pkg. miniature marshmallows
        1 pint whipping cream, whipped
        English walnuts (garnish)
        Lettuce leaves (garnish)

Mix together cranberries and sugar. Add grapes and marshmallows
to mixture. Fold in whipping cream. Cover and chill in
refrigerator overnight before serving.

WHEN READY TO SERVE - Serve on lettuce leaves and top with
walnuts.

CRANBERRY SALAD

Serves 12

        2 pkgs. cherry Jell-O
          Dissolve in 2 Cups boiling water, and cool
        2 tsp. lemon juice
        2 cans cranberry sauce (jelly)
        1 small can crushed pineapple
        1 pint sour cream
        1 Cup nuts, chopped

Add remaining ingredients to cooled Jell-O mixture, cover and
refrigerate overnight.

This is wonderful for Thanksgiving Dinner!

CROCK CABBAGE SALAD   Serves 6-8

Grind or chop:

1 medium head cabbage
4 carrots
2 red peppers
2 green peppers
2 large onions
1 tsp. celery seed

Soak all ingredients in salted water for 2 hours. Drain.

DRESSING   1 cup vinegar
                  2 1/2 Cups sugar

Mix well and pour over ingredients. Let stand in crock overnight
in refrigerator.

CUCUMBER SALAD MOLD   Serves 6-8

                1 (3 oz.) pkg. lime gelatin
                   Dissolve in 1 Cup boiling water
                1 Cup cucumber, peeled, diced and drained
                1/4 Cup cold water
                1 Tbsp. vinegar
                1/2 tsp. onion, grated
                1 (3 oz.) carton cream cheese, softened
                1 Cup celery, diced
                1/4 Cup green pepper, diced
                Lettuce leaves (garnish)

Stir in cucumber, cold water, vinegar and onion into dissolved
gelatin mixture. Pour half of cucumber mixture into a lightly
oiled 4-cup mold and chill until set.

Combine cream cheese and remaining cucumber mixture, stirring
well. Add celery and green pepper, mix well. Pour over cucumber
layer in mold. Chill overnight.

WHEN READY TO SERVE - Unmold and serve on lettuce leaves.

CUCUMBER-BEAN SALAD   Serves 8

                1 (10 oz.) pkg. frozen petite peas
                1 (10 oz.) pkg. frozen baby lima beans
                2 (3 oz.) pkgs. cream cheese, cubed
                1 med. cucumber, chopped
                1 small onion, chopped
                1/4 Cup mayonnaise or salad dressing

Cook lima beans and peas according to directions, drain and let
cool to room temperature. Combine vegetables and remaining
ingredients. Stir gently until well blended. Chill in
refrigerator overnight.

CURRY NUT SALAD   Serves 6

```
        1 Cup celery, diced
        1 large red bell pepper, julienne strips
        1 Cup raw frozen peas (if fresh, barely cook)
        1 head lettuce, cut up into small pieces
```

Mix together and store tightly covered in refrigerator.

GARNISH: 1 Tbsp. pine nuts
                1/2 tsp. capers

WHEN READY TO SERVE: Toss salad with Curry-Orange dressing (see Salad Dressings) and put on separate salad plates. Top with nuts and capers.

People rave about this salad.

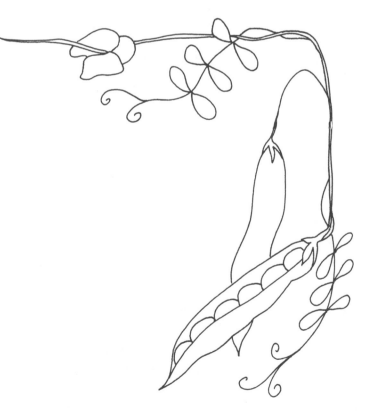

CURRIED SHRIMP AND CRAB SALAD   Serves 8-10

                1 (6 oz.) pkg. white and wild rice
                2 Cups shrimp, cleaned and cooked
                1 (6 oz.) pkg. frozen crab, thawed and drained
                1 Cup celery, diced
                1/2 Cup green pepper, diced
                1/4 Cup green onion, diced
                1 small can water chestnuts, diced
                1 bunch green grapes
                1/2 Cup whipped cream
                3/4 Cup mayonnaise
                1 tsp. curry powder
                2 tsp. fresh lemon juice
                Lettuce leaves (garnish)

Cook rice according to directions and cool. Reserve a few shrimp
for garnish. Combine remaining shrimp, crab, rice, celery, onion,
green pepper, water chestnuts and grapes. Mix together whipped
cream, mayonnaise, curry powder and lemon juice. Stir into rice
mixture. Cover and chill overnight in refrigerator.

WHEN READY TO SERVE - Spoon on lettuce leaves and garnish with
shrimp.

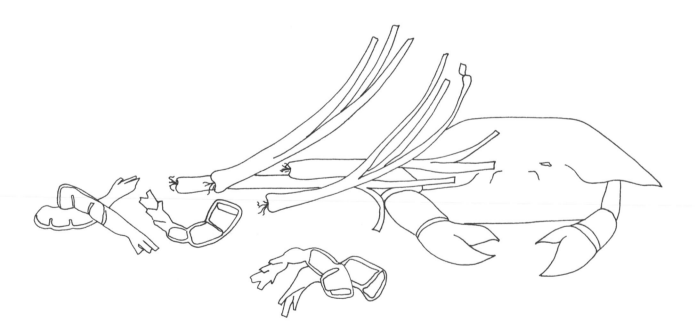

EMERALD SALAD   Serves 10-12

MARINATED SHRIMP: 1 lb. shrimp, cooked and cleaned
                       2 onions, cut into thinly sliced rings
                       1 Cup French dressing

Mix and chill all together. Chill in refrigerator overnight.

SALAD: 2 pkgs. lime Jell-O
                         Dissolve in 1 1/2 Cups boiling water
                       1 1/2 Cups cold water
                       1 1/2 Cups diced cucumber
                       1 tsp. salt
                       1/2 Cup vinegar
                       2 avocados
                       2 Tbsp. lemon juice
                       1 Cup small cocktail onions, halved
                       1 Cup stuffed green olives, halved

Add cold water to dissolved Jell-O. Marinate cucumber in vinegar
and salt. Remove seeds and skin of avocados and set aside one
half avocado. Cut 1 1/2 avocados into cubes, sprinkle with salt
and lemon juice. When Jell-O is slightly thickened, add drained
cucumbers, onion, olives and avocado cubes. Toss lightly and pour
into a wet ring mold. Cover and chill overnight.

WHEN READY TO SERVE - Unmold onto lettuce and fill center of mold
with marinated shrimp and surround with avocado slices. Pour
Louie Dressing over salad and shrimp. (See Salad Dressings)

Very delicious.

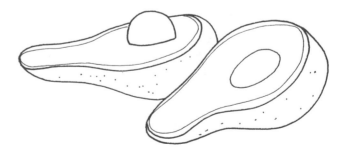

ENGLISH PEA SALAD   Serves 12

1 (15 oz.) can shoe peg corn, drained
1 (15 oz.) can tiny peas, drained
1 Cup celery, diced
1 med. bell green pepper, chopped
1 bunch green onions, chopped
1 cup pimentos, chopped
Lettuce leaves (garnish)

Mix vegetables together and set aside.

MARINADE: 1/2 Cup oil
                1/2 Cup wine vinegar
                1/2 Cup sugar
                1 Tbsp. salt
                1 Tbsp. water
                1 tsp. pepper
                1 tsp. celery seed

Mix all ingredients together and pour over vegetables. Cover
vegetables and allow to marinate in refrigerator overnight.

WHEN READY TO SERVE - Serve on a leaf of lettuce.

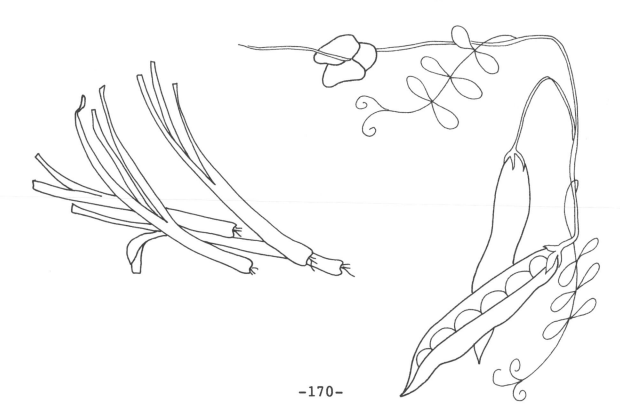

FIVE-STAR SALAD   Serves 8-10

      1 Cup mandarin orange segments, drained
      1 Cup pineapple chunks, drained
      1 Cup flaked coconut
      1 Cup miniature marshmallows
      1 Cup sour cream

Mix all ingredients together and chill overnight in refrigerator,
covered.

FROZEN DATE CREAM SALAD   Serves 8

                1 (8 oz.) pkg. cream cheese
                1 Cup maple syrup
                1 tsp. vanilla
                1 can crushed pineapple, drained
                1 Cup dates, chopped
                1 Cup nuts, chopped
                1/2 pint whipping cream

Beat cream cheese and syrup together. Add vanilla, pineapple,
dates and nuts. Whip cream and fold into mixture. Put in freezer
for 24 hours.

WHEN READY TO SERVE - To serve, cut in squares. It is a nice
salad to serve with ham.

It will keep in freezer for a month.

EASY FROZEN FRUIT SALAD   Serves 8

                1 can cherry pie filling
                1 can Eagle Brand milk
                1 large can crushed pineapple
                1 large carton whipped topping
                1 cup nuts, chopped

Mix all ingredients together and pour into loaf pan. Cover with
foil and freeze for 24 hours.

WHEN READY TO SERVE - Unmold and serve slices.

GREEN BEAN - RED POTATO SALAD   Serves 6-8

          12 small red potatoes, unpeeled
          1 lb. fresh green beans
          1 small red onion, sliced into rings and separated
          1 med. green pepper, sliced into rings
          1/2 Cup celery, diced
          1/4 Cup olive oil
          1/4 Cup fresh parsley, minced
          3 Tbsp. vinegar
          1/2 tsp. salt
          1/4 tsp. pepper
          1/8 tsp. dried oregano
          Lettuce leaves or endive (garnish)

Cook potatoes in boiling water for 20 minutes or until tender.
Drain and cool. Thinly slice potatoes and set aside.

Remove strings from beans and cut into 1" pieces. Wash
thoroughly. Cover and cook in boiling water for 10-15 minutes or
until beans are crisp and tender. Drain and cool. Combine
potatoes, green beans, onion, green pepper and celery in a mixing
bowl. Combine next 6 ingredients in a jar, cover and shake
vigorously. Pour over vegetables and toss gently. Cover tightly
and chill in refrigerator overnight.

WHEN READY TO SERVE - Place salad on bed of lettuce leaves or
endive.

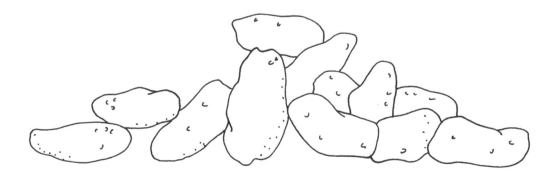

ITALIAN SPAGHETTI SALAD   Serves 12

                1 1/4 lb. broken spaghetti, cooked and drained
                1/2 Cup green pepper, diced
                1/4 Cup red onion, chopped
                1/4 Cup pimentos, diced
                1 (15 1/2 oz.) jar spaghetti sauce
                1/4 Cup black olives, sliced
                2 firm tomatoes, diced
                1 large cucumber, diced
                1 pkg. dry Italian season mix
                2 (8 oz.) bottles Italian dressing
                Salt and pepper to taste

Combine cooked spaghetti with remaining ingredients, saving 1
bottle of Italian dressing out to use at time of serving. Toss
gently, cover and chill overnight.

WHEN READY TO SERVE - Add second bottle of dressing and toss
gently.

This is wonderful for a big patio party on a warm evening.

24-HOUR KRAUT SALAD   Serves 8-10

       1 large can kraut, adding a little water.
       1 Cup celery, chopped
       1 Cup onion, chopped
       1/2 Cup green pepper, chopped

Boil kraut with a little water for 15 minutes. Rinse in cold water until cool, drain and chop. Add celery, onion and green pepper and mix well.

DRESSING: 1/2 Cup oil
               1/2 Cup vinegar
               1 Cup sugar

Heat until sugar dissolves.

Pour dressing over vegetables and toss gently. Cover bowl and chill overnight.

This will keep in refrigerator for 7-10 days.

LIME PARTY SALAD   Serves 8-10

        1/4 lb. marshmallows, 16 count
        1 Cup milk
        1 (6 oz.) pkg. lime Jell-O
        2 (3 oz.) pkgs. cream cheese
        1 (#2) can crushed pineapple, undrained
        2/3 Cup mayonnaise
        1 Cup whipping cream, (whipped)

Melt marshmallows and milk in double boiler. Add Jell-O and stir
until dissolved. Add cream cheese and stir until dissolved. Add
pineapple and mix well. Cool. Blend in mayonnaise. Fold in
whipped cream, cover and chill in refrigerator overnight.

Excellent salad for Christmas holiday buffet.

MANDARIN ORANGE MOLDED SALAD   Serves 8

        1 can mandarin oranges, drained
        1 small pkg. orange Jell-O
          Dissolve in 1 Cup boiling water
        1 Cup orange juice
        2 Tbsp. lime juice
        1 large pkg. cream cheese, cut into cubes

Add orange and lime juice to warm Jell-O. Add cream cheese to
jell-O mixture and stir until creamy. In an 8" square Pyrex dish,
arrange mandarin oranges on bottom of dish. Pour half of Jell-O
mixture on top of layered oranges and chill in refrigerator until
congealed. Then, pour remaining Jell-O and cover. Refrigerate
overnight before serving.

MACARONI SALAD   Serves 6

        8 oz. pkg. elbow macaroni, cooked and drained
        1 tsp. crushed garlic
        1 Tbsp. lemon juice
        1/2 Cup mayonnaise
        1 small can garbanzo beans, drained
        1 (8 oz.) jar stuffed green olives, cut in half
        1 dill pickle, chopped
        1/2 Cup onion, chopped

Mix mayonnaise and lemon juice together, add remaining
ingredients, cover and chill overnight in refrigerator.

WHEN READY TO SERVE - Serve in a lettuce lined bowl.

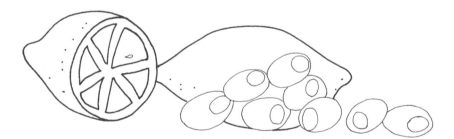

MEXICAN ORANGE AND ONION SALAD   Serves 8

        2 oranges, peeled and slice into paper thin circles
        1 red onion, slice into paper thin rings
        16 pitted black olives
        Tart French dressing (see Salad Dressings)
        Lettuce leaves

Pour tart French dressing over orange slices, onion rings and
olives. Cover and chill in refrigerator overnight.

WHEN READY TO SERVE - Attractively arrange on lettuce leaves.

NEXT DAY VEGETABLE SALAD   Serves 8-10

       1/2 medium head cauliflower, cut into pieces
       1/2 large bunch broccoli, cut into pieces
       1 med. head lettuce, bite size pieces
       1 lb. bacon, cooked crisp and crumbled
       1 med. red onion, sliced into thin rings
       1/4 Cup grated Parmesan cheese
       2 Cups mayonnaise
       1 Tbsp. sugar
       Dash of white pepper
       Shredded lettuce (garnish)
       1 green onion, finely chopped (garnish)

Layer: cauliflower, broccoli, lettuce, bacon, onion and cheese in a 4 quart glass bowl. Repeat to top. Sprinkle sugar on top. Combine mayonnaise with salt and pepper and spread evenly over top, sealing salad to edge of bowl. Cover tightly and refrigerate overnight.

WHEN READY TO SERVE - Garnish top of salad with shredded lettuce and green onion.

OKLAHOMA SLAW   Serves 8-10

     1 large head cabbage, shredded
     1 large onion, chopped
     1 Cup sugar
     1 Cup vinegar
     3/4 Cup oil
     1 Tbsp. dry mustard or mustard seed
     1 tsp. celery seed

Toss together cabbage and onion. Place in a large bowl. Sprinkle
sugar on top. Do not stir. Boil vinegar, oil, dry mustard and
celery seed together. Pour over cabbage mixture. Do not stir.
Cover quickly and chill in refrigerator overnight.

OVERNIGHT FIESTA SALAD   Serves 6-8

     1 (15 1/2 oz.) can kidney beans, drained
     1 med. onion, chopped
     2 med. tomatoes, unpeeled and coarsely chopped
     1/2 Cup celery, diced
     1/2 Cup green pepper, chopped
     1/2 Cup French dressing
     1 small head iceberg lettuce, bite-size pieces
     1 Cup cheddar cheese, grated
     3 hard cooked eggs, chopped
     1 Cup crushed corn chips (garnish)

In a large bowl layer first 9 ingredients in order listed. Cover
tightly and refrigerate overnight.

WHEN READY TO SERVE - Toss gently and garnish with crushed corn
chips.

OVERNIGHT TOSSED SALAD   Serves 12

                1 med. head iceberg lettuce,
                   cut into bite size pieces
                1 bunch fresh spinach,
                   cut into bite size pieces
                1/2 Cup green olives, sliced
                1 pint cherry tomatoes, halved
                1 lb. bacon, cooked crisp and crumbled

Layer above ingredients in a large salad bowl.

DRESSING: 1 1/2 Cup mayonnaise
                1 Cup sour cream
                2 Tbsp. lemon juice
                1/2 tsp. oregano leaves, crushed
                1/4 tsp. basil leaves, crushed
                Salt and pepper to taste

Combine dressing ingredients and mix well. Spread dressing over
top of salad, making sure entire surface is covered to edge of
bowl. Cover tightly and chill in refrigerator overnight.

WHEN READY TO SERVE - Toss lightly.

PERFECTION SALAD   Serves 6

      1 pkg. unflavored gelatin
      1/4 cup cold water
      1 Cup very hot water
      1/4 Cup sugar
      1/2 tsp. salt
      1 Tbsp. lemon juice
      1/4 Cup vinegar
      1/2 Cup cabbage, finely shredded
      1 Cup celery, finely diced
      1 pimento, finely chopped
      2 Tbsp. sweet red or green pepper, finely chopped
      1/2 Cup carrots, finely chopped
      Parsley, chopped

Sprinkle gelatin in cold water in top of double boiler to soften.
Add hot water, sugar and salt. Stir over boiling water until
thoroughly dissolved. Add the lemon juice and vinegar. Chill
until mixture is the consistency of unbeaten egg whites. Add
vegetables, mix and pour into a slightly oiled mold. Cover and
chill overnight in refrigerator.

WHEN READY TO SERVE - Unmold on salad green, garnish with a dollop
of mayonnaise or you can cut into cubes and serve in green pepper
shells.

PINEAPPLE SOUR CREAM SALAD   Serves 6-8

> 1 pkg lemon Jell-O
> 1/2 tsp. salt
>   Dissolve above 2 ingredients in 1 Cup hot water
> 1/4 Cup cold water
> 2 Tbsp. lemon juice
> 1 Cup sour cream
> 1 1/2 Cups canned crushed pineapple, drained

Add cold water, add lemon juice and sour cream to Jell-O mixture.
Beat until blended. Set in ice water to chill. Beat until thick
and foamy. Fold in pineapple. Chill in refrigerator covered
overnight.

RED CABBAGE SALAD   Serves 6-8

> 1/2 head of red cabbage, shredded
> 1/2 Cup oil
> 1/2 Cup plus 2 Tbsp. red wine vinegar
> 3 Tbsp. sugar
> 1 tsp. salt
> 1 tsp. seasoned salt
> 1/4 tsp. black pepper
> 1/4 tsp. onion powder

Shred cabbage so it is irregular, some fine and some coarse shreds
into bowl. Add remaining ingredients and mix well. Let stand for
overnight to allow flavors to mellow and slaw to achieve a deep
red color.

If you have one serving, you will definitely want more!

RICE SALAD   Serves 4-6

         1 Cup brown rice
         2 1/2 Cups chicken broth
           or bouillon cubes with water
         2 (6 oz.) jars artichoke hearts
            with liquid, chopped
         1/2 green pepper, chopped
         3 green onions, chopped
         10 stuffed olives with pimentos, sliced
         1/2 tsp. curry powder (or more to taste)
         1/3 Cup mayonnaise

Cook rice in chicken broth and cool. Mix all ingredients
together, alternating the amount of artichoke juice and mayonnaise
to get the consistency you desire. You can add cooked chicken,
chopped or shrimp to make a main dish.

To make for a larger crowd, I usually double the recipe.

RICE-VEGETABLE SALAD   Serves 6

         1/2 Cup Italian dressing
         3/4 Cup water
         1 Cup instant rice, uncooked
         1 can English peas, drained
         4 green onions, sliced with tops
         1/4 Cup stuffed green olives, sliced
         1/4 Cup peeled cucumber, diced
         1 Cup cheddar cheese, coarsely grated
         1 hard cooked egg, sliced (garnish)
         Lettuce leaves (garnish)

Bring to a boil one half of dressing and water in a medium
saucepan. Stir in rice, cover and remove from heat. Let stand
for 5 minutes. Combine rice, remaining dressing and ingredients,
mix well, cover and chill overnight in refrigerator.

WHEN READY TO SERVE - Garnish with sliced egg and serve on lettuce
leaves.

ST. PATRICK'S DAY SALAD   Serves 8

        1/2 Cup water
        1 can cream of asparagus soup
        2 Tbsp. onion, grated or chopped
        1/2 Cup mayonnaise
        1/2 Cup green pepper
        1 (3 oz.) pkg. lime Jell-O
        1 (8 oz.) pkg. cream cheese, cut into cubes
        1/2 Cup pecans, chopped
        3/4 Cup celery, chopped

Heat soup, water and Jell-O until dissolved. DO NOT BOIL. Stir
well, add cream cheese cubes. Some bits of cheese should be seen.
Add rest of ingredients and pour into lightly oiled mold. Chill
in refrigerator over night.

WHEN READY TO SERVE - Unmold salad onto a lettuce lined serving
plate.

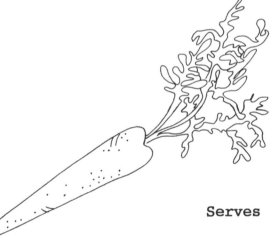

SALAD BALLS   Serves 8

        4 carrots, grated
        1/2 Cup peanut butter
        1/2 Cup raisins
        1/2 Cup mayonnaise
        Lettuce leaves (garnish)

Mix ingredients together and roll into balls. Chill in
refrigerator overnight.

WHEN READY TO SERVE - Serve on lettuce leaves for a salad or
snack.

CURRIED SEAFOOD SALAD   Serves 4-6

                    1 can tuna
                    1 Cup shrimp, cleaned and cooked
                    1/2 Cup mayonnaise
                    2 Tbsp. lemon juice
                    2-3 Tbsp. French dressing
                    1 tsp. curry powder
                    1/2 Cup celery, chopped
                    1/2 Cup olives, chopped
                    3 Cups rice, cooked
                    1/2 Cup parsley, minced

Drain tuna well. In a large bowl combine shrimp and tuna, add
celery and 1/4 cup olives. In a small bowl blend mayonnaise,
curry powder and lemon juice. Pour over tuna and shrimp mixture,
toss, cover and refrigerate overnight. In another bowl mix French
dressing with rice and parsley, cover and chill overnight in
refrigerator.

WHEN READY TO SERVE - Spoon rice onto a serving platter, making
mound. Heap seafood mixture on top and garnish with remaining
olives.

SHRIMP MOLDED SALAD   Serves 8-10

> 2 Tbsp. unflavored gelatin in 1/2 Cup cold water
> 1 can tomato soup with 1 can water added
> 3 (3 oz.) pkgs. cream cheese
> 2 Tbsp. mayonnaise
> 1 cucumber, chopped
> 1 onion, chopped
> 1/3 green pepper, chopped
> 2 hard cooked eggs
> 2 stalks celery, chopped
> 1/2 lb. small bay shrimp

Bring soup to boil, add gelatin mixture and stir. Remove from heat. When cool add cheese and mayonnaise. Blend in blender at high speed.

In a large bowl, add remaining ingredients and stir well. Pour into a lightly oiled mold and chill overnight.

DRESSING - 1/2 Cup sour cream and 1/2 Cup mayonnaise.

Delicious.

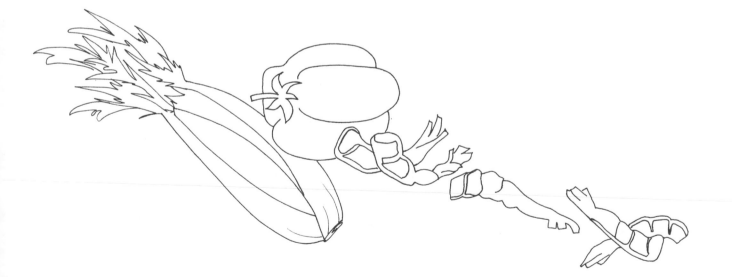

SPAGHETTI FRUIT SALAD   Serves 8-10

> 1/2 lb. extra thin spaghetti,
>   cooked, drained and cool
> 2 apples, peeled and diced
> 1 Cup canned pineapple chunks, drained
> 1 Cup mandarin oranges, drained
> 1/2 Cup coconut
> 1 Cup whipped cream or whipped topping

DRESSING - 2 eggs, beaten
          1/4 Cup lemon juice
          1 Cup powdered sugar

Mix eggs, powdered sugar and lemon juice together. Cook in heavy pan, stirring until thick. Cool.

Fold cooled spaghetti and fruit into cooled dressing. Chill overnight in the refrigerator. Before serving fold in 1 cup of whipped cream or whipped topping.

A nice salad for a ladies bridge luncheon.

TOMATO SOUP SALAD   Serves 8-10

        2 cans tomato soup
        2 (3 oz.) pkgs. lemon Jell-O
        1 (#2) can crushed pineapple
        1 Cup celery, diced
        Juice of 2 lemons
        Lettuce leaves (garnish)
        Mayonnaise (garnish)
        Parsley (garnish)

Heat soup. DO NOT BOIL. Add Jell-O and dissolve. Pour into bowl
and add juice, pineapple and celery. Pour into a lightly oiled
mold or an 8" x 12" lightly oiled dish. Cover and chill overnight
in refrigerator.

WHEN READY TO SERVE - Serve on lettuce leaves and garnish with
dollops of mayonnaise and a sprig of parsley.

MARINATED VEGETABLE SALAD   Serves 12

        1 can cut green beans, drained
        1 can kidney beans, drained
        1 can wax beans, drained
        1 can pitted ripe olives, drained
        1 small jar sliced mushrooms, drained
        1 small jar sliced pimentos, drained
        1 jar artichoke hearts, drained and quartered
        1 small onion, thinly sliced
        1/4 Cup vinegar
        1/4 Cup salad oil
        2 tsp. sugar
        Salt and pepper to taste

Combine vegetables in a large mixing bowl, toss lightly. Combine
remaining ingredients in a jar and shake vigorously. Pour
marinade over vegetables and chill overnight in refrigerator.

VEGETABLE-PASTA SALAD   Serves 8

1 lb. colored spiral pasta, cooked and drained
1 can black olives
1 Cup celery, chopped
1 Cup green onions, chopped
1 Cup carrots, blanched and sliced
1 Cup broccoli, blanched bite-size pieces
1 Cup cauliflower, blanched bite-size pieces
1 jar marinated artichokes
2 tomatoes, cut into bite-size pieces
1/2-1 Cup grated Parmesan cheese
1 (8 oz.) jar Italian salad dressing
1/2 Cup mayonnaise
1 can med. shrimp (optional)

Mix together first ten ingredients, add cheese (I like lots of
this), salad dressing and toss. Cover tightly and chill in
refrigerator overnight.

WHEN READY TO SERVE - Add mayonnaise to salad and if desired
shrimp, toss and serve.

This is a great salad to take to a potluck supper.

Salad
Dressings

CHILI SALAD DRESSING   Serves 6

        1 Cup French dressing, chilled
        1/2 Cup sour cream
        1/2 Cup green pepper, finely diced
        Dash of chili powder

Mix together and put in covered jar. Keep in refrigerator for at least 24 hours.

Serve over hearts of lettuce.

This will keep in the refrigerator for two weeks.

CREAM SALAD DRESSING   Serves 6

        2 egg yolks
        2 Tbsp. flour
        1/2 tsp. dry mustard
        1/2 tsp. salt
        2 Tbsp. sugar
        2 Tbsp. butter
        1/2 Cup vinegar and juice of 1 lemon
        1 Cup cream

Mix dry ingredients with eggs and butter. Heat vinegar and add to egg mixture and cook until thick. Remove from heat and add cream, beating until smooth. Last, add lemon juice or vinegar. Keep in covered jar for at least 24 hours in refrigerator.

Serve with fruit, slaw or vegetable salad.

CREME FRAICHE   Serve 6-8

      1 Cup heavy cream
      1 cup sour cream

Whisk heavy cream and sour cream together. Cover bowl loosely and let stand at room temperature overnight. Cover tightly and refrigerate until quite thick. The flavor will become tart as it sits in the refrigerator. It can be refrigerated for up to 2 weeks.

You can spoon this over fruit or berries. Add to sauces for more richness. Stir in by a spoonful to butter-warmed vegetables. It can be added to salad dressing to make it thicker.

When making additional batches of creme fraiche, substitute 1 Cup creme fraiche for sour cream.

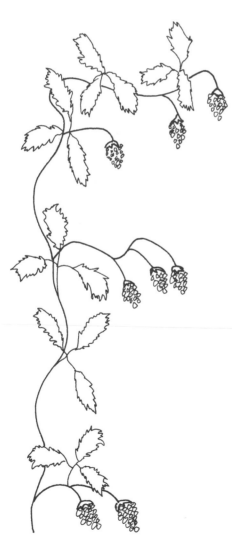

CUCUMBER DRESSING   Makes 2 quarts

> 1 quart Best Foods mayonnaise
> 1 large onion, chopped
> 1 large cucumber, chopped
> 1 tsp. Accent
> 1 small clove garlic
> Juice of 1 lemon
> Dash of Worcestershire sauce
> Salt to taste

Blend all ingredients in the blender or Cuisinart. Refrigerate until ready to use or overnight. Keeps well. Excellent over a tossed salad or sliced tomatoes.

CURRY-ORANGE DRESSING

> 8 oz. corn oil
> 1/4 Cup orange juice
> 1 tsp curry powder
> 1 Tbsp. orange rind, grated
> Salt and pepper to taste

Mix together and store covered in refrigerator overnight.

Serve with Curry Nut salad.

DILL DRESSING   Serves 6

>   1/2 Cup cottage cheese
>   1/2 Cup mayonnaise
>   1/2 Cup milk
>   1 Tbsp. olive oil
>   2 Tbsp. vinegar or lemon juice
>   1/8 tsp. sugar
>   Salt and pepper to taste
>   1 clove garlic, minced
>   1 tsp. dried dill weed

Blend together and place in covered jar. Chill in refrigerator overnight and serve over lettuce or spinach salad.

EVERYDAY SALAD DRESSING   Serves 6-8

>   2 Tbsp. sugar
>   2 Tbsp. ketchup
>   2 Tbsp. A-1 sauce
>   2 Tbsp. mayonnaise
>   2 Tbsp. salad oil
>   2 Tbsp. vinegar
>   1 Tbsp. Worcestershire sauce
>   1 tsp. onion salt
>   Pepper to taste

Blend all ingredients until perfectly smooth.

This can be made for a large crowd by using cups instead of tablespoons.

FRENCH DRESSING   Serves 6-8

> 1 can tomato soup
> 1 1/2 Cup sugar
> 1 tsp. salt
> 1 tsp. dry mustard
> 1 Tbsp. Worcestershire sauce
> 3/4 Cup vegetable oil
> 3/4 Cup vinegar

Place in covered jar and shake well. Garlic salt and more vinegar
may be added if a more tart dressing is desired.

Refrigerate overnight to enhance flavor. This is good on a mixed
green salad.

FRUIT SALAD DRESSING   Serves 4-6

> 1 can Eagle Brand milk
> 2 eggs, beaten
> 3/4 Cup vinegar
> 2 Tbsp. butter, melted
> 1 tsp. salt
> 1/2 tsp. dry mustard

Slowly add milk to beaten eggs and mix well. Add other
ingredients and blend.

Refrigerate overnight and serve with mixed fresh fruit.

ITALIAN DRESSING

- A -		- B -
1/2 tsp. oregano		1 Cup mayonnaise
1/2 Cup salad oil	or	1/2 Cup ketchup
1/2 Cup wine vinegar		1/2 Cup buttermilk
		1 tsp. garlic salt or
		Pinch of garlic powder
		1 tsp. paprika
		1/2 tsp. Worcestershire

Mix ingredients together and chill in refrigerator in tightly
sealed bottle.

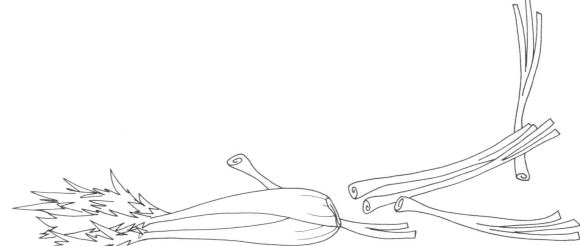

LOUIE DRESSING

1 1/2 Cups Best Foods mayonnaise
1/4 Cup chili sauce
1/2 Cup celery, minced
1/4 Cup scallions, minced
2 hard boiled eggs, diced
1/4 Cup pickle relish
1 Tbsp. parsley, minced
1 tsp. salt
1/2 tsp. pepper

Mix all ingredients together, put in the refrigerator overnight.

This is wonderful served over shrimp or crab salad.

OIL AND VINEGAR DRESSING   For 1 green salad

        4 Tbsp. salad oil
        2 Tbsp. sugar, heaping
        2 Tbsp. vinegar
        Salt and pepper to taste
        Dash of Paprika
        1/4 tsp. dry mustard

Mix in a covered jar and shake well. Store overnight in
refrigerator before serving over a green salad.

This will keep for several weeks in refrigerator

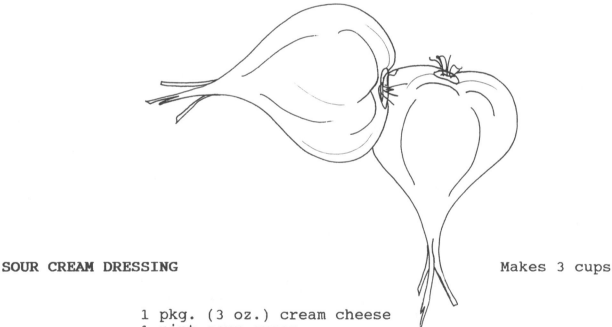

SOUR CREAM DRESSING   Makes 3 cups

        1 pkg. (3 oz.) cream cheese
        1 pint sour cream
        1 Tbsp. vegetable oil
        1 garlic clove, minced
        1 tsp. Worcestershire sauce

Place minced garlic in oil and let stand. Mix cheese and sour
cream, add salt, pepper and Worcestershire sauce. Add to oil
mixture and mix well. Chill overnight. Serve on green salad.

STEAK GROUP BLUE CHEESE DRESSING   Serves 12

        1 pint sour cream
        1 tsp. fresh lemon juice
        1 tsp. Worcestershire sauce
        1/2 Cup blue cheese, crumbled
        1 tsp. seasoning salt

Mix and store in covered jar in refrigerator overnight.

Serve on lettuce salad and top with ground pepper.

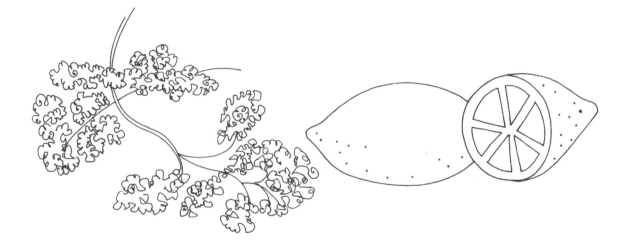

TARTAR SAUCE   Serves 8-10

        1 quart Best Foods mayonnaise
        2 Cups onion, chopped
        1/2 Cup dill pickles, chopped
        1/4 cup parsley, finely chopped
        1/4 bottle capers, chopped
        Juice of 1 lemon
        1/2 tsp. salt
        1/2 tsp. dill seed

Mix together and store in a covered container in the refrigerator
overnight before serving with fish, etc.

This will keep in the refrigerator for several weeks.

Side Dishes and Sauces

BAKED CURRIED FRUIT   Serves 12

                1 - (#303) can Cling peach halves
                1 - (#2) can pineapple slices
                1 - (#303) can pear halves
                1/3 Cup butter, melted
                3/4 Cup light brown sugar
                4 tsp. curry powder
                5 maraschino cherries with stems (garnish)
                Parsley sprigs (garnish)

DAY BEFORE - Drain canned fruit, dry well on toweling. Arrange in
1 1/2 quart casserole. Mix together melted butter, sugar and
curry powder. Spoon over fruit. Bake @ 325° for 1 hour -
uncovered. Remove, cover and refrigerate overnight.

THIRTY MINUTES BEFORE SERVING - Reheat casserole in 350° oven for
30 minutes. Garnish with parsley and Maraschino cherries. Serve
with ham, lamb, poultry, etc.

BAKED ORANGES

                4 to 5 Navel oranges

Boil whole for 45 minutes. Then, section them into 1" wedges and
arrange in a baking dish.

SYRUP   1 Cup sugar
                1/2 Cup orange juice
                2 tsp. corn syrup
                Few drops of red food coloring

Pour syrup over oranges. Bake for 45 minutes at 325°. Allow to
cool and store covered in refrigerator.

Delicious served with fowl or pork.

CRANBERRY AND ORANGE RELISH

> 4 Cups cranberries (1 lb.)
> 2 large oranges
> 2 Cups sugar

Grind cranberries and oranges together and mix with sugar. Chill
overnight. Remember this relish for Thanksgiving Day. It will
keep in a covered container in the refrigerator for several weeks.

CRANBERRY CORDIAL

> 4 Cups cranberries - coarse ground
> 3 Cups sugar
> 2 Cups Gin or Vodka

Place in large screw top jar. Add sugar and Gin or Vodka. Cover
tightly and invert jar. Let stand 24 hours. Then shake jar daily
for 3 weeks. Strain through cheesecloth. Cover. Spoon drained
berries into covered container and refrigerate. Use berries in
muffins, cake or spoon over ice cream.

Juice can be refrigerated in a covered jar also, to be used as a
liqueur or mixed with fresh fruit.

MARINATED CARROTS
Cold vegetable

                    2 lbs. fresh carrots, peeled and sliced -
                    or - 1 1/2 lbs. frozen carrots

Boil 5 to 10 minutes until semi-tender. (They soften in marinade
a little.) Drain well and cool slightly

MARINADE   Mix together:

                  1 small green pepper, chopped
                  4 green onions, chopped
                  1 can tomato soup
                  1/2 Cup salad oil
                  1 Cup sugar
                  3/4 Cup white vinegar
                  1 tsp. prepared mustard
                  1 tsp. Worcestershire sauce
                  Black pepper to taste

Pour marinade over carrots and refrigerate. Will keep several
days to one week in refrigerator.

DEVONSHIRE CREAM SAUCE

     1 pint whipping cream
     1 Cup sour cream
     1/2 Cup powdered sugar
     2 oz. Grand Marnier or Apry (apricot liqueur)

Whip heavy cream until just thickened. Slowly fold in sour cream.
Continue whipping until smooth. Stir in sugar, lemon juice and
liqueur.

Spread on scones.

GOVERNOR SAUCE   Yield: 12-14 pints

            8 quarts tomatoes, chopped
            5 sweet red peppers, chopped
            7 large onions, chopped
            3 large apples, cored, peeled and chopped
            5 Cups vinegar
            5 Tbsp. salt
            1 Tbsp. cinnamon
            1 Tbsp. cloves
            4 Cups sugar

Place all ingredients, except sugar in a very large sauce pot and
boil for one hour. Add 4 Cups sugar and stir well. Pour into
sterilized jars and seal.

This is an old family recipe to be used as a meat sauce. It is
wonderful. This used to be a Woodward's secret recipe.

LEMON CURD (or LIME)   Yield: 1 quart

            8 ozs. sugar
            4 eggs
            Juice of 4 lemons
            Grated rind of 2 lemons
            4 ozs. sweet butter, cut into pieces

Whisk eggs and sugar together. Add lemon juice, lemon rind and
butter. Cook in double boiler, stirring from time to time until
the curd thickens - about 20-30 minutes.

Pour thickened curd into hot sterilized jars. Cover and seal
while hot. Let cool overnight. Should be eaten within one month.

This is a traditional English Christmas treat.

PICKLED FIGS

>   36 fresh figs
>   2 Tbsp. salt
>   1 gallon water

Wash figs. Place in salted water. Bring to boil. Turn off heat
and let stand for 5 minutes. Drain in colander and lift out
carefully.

SYRUP: 5 Cups sugar
                2 Cups water
                1/2 - 1 Cup vinegar
                Cloves (to liking)
                1 Cinnamon stick

Bring syrup of sugar, water and vinegar to boil. Drop figs in
carefully. Cook approximately 5 minutes. Let stand overnight.

This process takes three days. Second day repeat. Third day add
cloves to your liking and one stick of cinnamon. Bring to boil
and can. Put in jars and seal lids.

PINEAPPLE SIDE DISH   (For ham)

     2 Cups (8 oz.) pineapple chunks, drain and save
       liquid
     2 Cups cheddar cheese, grated
     2 Cups Ritz crackers, crushed
     2 cubes butter, melted
     6 Tbsp. pineapple juice
     6 Tbsp. flour
     2 Cups sugar

Mix flour and sugar and heat until sugar melts. Mix pineapple
chunks and cheese in greased Pyrex (9" square). Add liquid
mixture and mix well. Spread crushed crackers over all and
drizzle melted butter on top. This can be covered and
refrigerated overnight.

Bake at 350° for 30 minutes before serving.

SECRET SALMON SAUCE   (Also delicious on chicken)

        1 cube butter or margarine, melted
        4 Cups brown sugar
        1 Cup lemon juice
        1 tsp. dill weed
        2 dashes cayenne red pepper

Stir in brown sugar and lemon juice to melted butter. Add dill
and pepper and mix well. The consistency should be about as thick
as pancake batter. If too thick, add more lemon juice. If too
thin add more brown sugar.

Sauce should be applied to salmon or chicken about a minute or so
before it has finished cooking.

STRAWBERRY BUTTER

        1 (10 oz.) pkg. frozen strawberries, thawed
        1 Cup butter or margarine, softened
        1 Cup powdered sugar

In the blender combine strawberries, butter and powdered sugar.
Can store in refrigerator for several days.

This is a delicious spread for biscuits or muffins or it will add
a new taste treat when used on French bread or waffles.

SPICED VEGETABLES

                4 carrots, scraped and cut into small pieces
                4 stalks celery, cut into small pieces
                1 small head cauliflower, cut into small pieces
                1/2 lb. small fresh mushrooms
                4 cloves garlic, minced
                1 Tbsp. salt
                3 Cups water
                1/2 cup vinegar
                1 Tbsp. mixed pickling spices
                1 1/2 tsp. whole dill seed
                1 tsp. whole mustard seed

Prepare vegetables and place in bowl with garlic and salt.
Combine other ingredients in sauce pan and bring to boil. Let
cool and pour over vegetables. Refrigerate a day or two. Drain
and serve as a side dish with dip.

DIP   1 pint sour cream
                1 mashed avocado
                Lemon juice
                1/4 Cup onion, finely chopped
                2 tsp. salt
                1/4 tsp. sugar
                1 tsp. Worcestershire
                4 dashes Tabasco sauce

Mix together. Cover and chill in refrigerator.

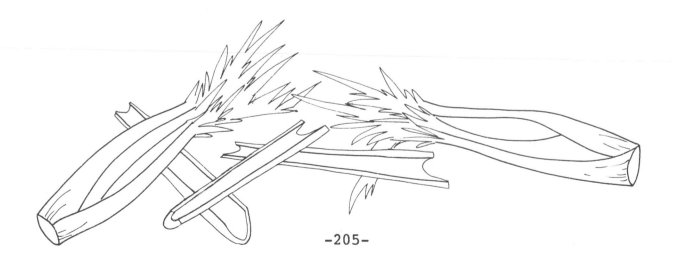

SWEET AND SOUR CUCUMBER CHIPS   Yield: 3 1/2 cups

        2 large cucumbers, peeled and sliced 1/4" thick
        3/4 tsp. salt, sprinkle over cucumbers

Let stand for two hours. Drain well and place in medium bowl.

        Add:

        1/2 Cup green pepper, diced 1/4" thick
        1/2 Cup onion, thinly sliced

        Combine:

        1/2 Cup white vinegar
        1/2 Cup plus 2 Tbsp. sugar
        1 1/2 tsp. celery seed

Stir until sugar is dissolved. Pour over cucumbers and
refrigerate at least two days. May keep several months in
refrigerator.

MARINATED ZUCCHINI WITH TOMATOES   4-5 servings

                    1 lb. (2 cups) zucchini, thinly sliced
                    1/2 Cup cream-style cottage cheese
                    2 - 3 Tbsp. chives, finely chopped
                    1/4 Cup sour cream
                    1/2 tsp. garlic salt
                    1 Tbsp. lemon juice
                    1/4 Cup green pepper, bite size
                    2 tomatoes, sliced

Cook zucchini in boiling water until tender - crispy (2-3 minutes). Drain very well. Combine cottage cheese, sour cream, lemon juice and garlic salt. Add zucchini and green pepper. Toss to coat. Chill and serve on tomato slices on a lettuce lined platter.

ZUCCHINI PICKLES

                    1 lb. zucchini, thinly sliced
                    1/4 lb. onion (approximately 3), thinly sliced
                    2 Tbsp. salt

MIX: 1/2 Cup sugar (or 1/3 cup honey)
                    1/2 tsp. celery seed
                    1/2 tsp. dry mustard
                    1/2 tsp. mustard seed
                    1 Cup cider vinegar

Place thinly sliced zucchini and onion rings in medium sauce pan. Cover with cold water and salt and let stand for one hour. Bring to a boil and boil for 3 minutes. Turn into jars and add other ingredients. Cover tightly and refrigerate at least overnight.

BLANCHED VEGETABLES   Serves 10-12

     1 Cup broccoli - wash and cut into small pieces
     1 Cup cauliflower - wash and cut into small pieces
     1 Cup string beans-wash and remove strings, leave whole
     1 Cup snow peas - wash and remove strings
     1 small bunch carrots - clean and cut into strips
     1 small bunch asparagus-wash and remove bottom of stems

Individually blanch each vegetable in double boiler for 2-3
minutes. After blanching, dip vegetables in ice water and drain.
Chill vegetables in covered container in refrigerator overnight.

Serve on large serving platter or basket along with cherry
tomatoes, green pepper slices and fresh sliced mushrooms.

Flavor 1 cup mayonnaise with 1 tsp. curry powder and serve as a
topping for the blanched vegetables.

This is not only a very colorful dish to serve but is also healthy
and delicious.

Soups

PROVINCIAL BEAN SOUP   Makes - 3 quarts

```
1 lb. (2 Cups) Navy beans
6 Cups water
1 Cup onion, chopped
2 Cups carrots, sliced
3 leeks (white part sliced)
2 cloves garlic, minced
2 Tbsp. vegetable oil
2 lb. ham hock
1/2 Cup fresh parsley, chopped
2 Bay leaves
Salt and pepper to taste
1 tsp. thyme
4 whole cloves
2 Cups sweet potatoes, pared and cubed
2 Cups turnips, pared and cubed
2 Cups green cabbage, shredded
6 additional cups of water
```

Bring to boil in a large pan, beans and 6 Cups water. Boil for 2 minutes and remove from heat. Let stand for one hour.

In the soup kettle, saute onion, carrots, leeks, garlic in oil until wilted. Add ham hock to kettle, add beans and liquid, stir in remaining water and seasonings. Cook for 1 1/2 hours over low heat. Add sweet potatoes, turnips and green cabbage and bring to boil. Cover and cook for an additional hour or until tender. Remove ham hock, cut meat into small pieces and return to soup.

Chill in refrigerator overnight and heat before serving the next day.

Really delicious.

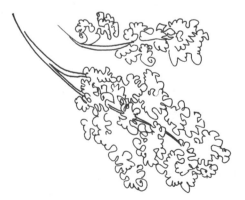

BLEU CHEESE SOUP   Serves 4

        2 Tbsp. margarine
        2 Tbsp. flour
        2 (10 oz.) cans chicken broth
        1 Cup bleu cheese, crumbled
        1/2 Tbsp. dried chopped onions
        1 Tbsp. whipped cream (garnish)
        Parsley, chopped (garnish)

Melt margarine and stir in flour to make a gravy. Add chicken
broth to gravy in one half cup portions to desired thickness. Add
crumbled bleu cheese and dried onions. Let stand overnight to
thicken.

Re-warm to serve, and garnish with parsley and a dollop of whipped
cream.

BROCCOLI SOUP   Serves 4

        4 small potatoes, cooked
        4 tsp. butter
        4 Tbsp. cooked rice
        4 Tbsp. sour cream
        1 clove garlic, minced
        1 onion, minced
        1 can chicken consomme
        2 stems broccoli, peeled cut into small pieces
        Salt and pepper to taste

Cook broccoli for 5 to 6 minutes in boiling water. Save 1/2 cup
of broccoli water. Place in blender, add remaining ingredients
and whip at high speed. Cover and chill in refrigerator
overnight.

WHEN READY TO SERVE - Stir continually while reheating the next
day.

BEEF SOUP   Serves 6

                1 1/2 lbs. lean ground beef
                1 large onion, chopped
                5 stalks celery, diced
                2 medium cans kidney beans, drained
                1 large can tomatoes
                1 large can water
                1 tsp. chili powder
                1/2 head cabbage, finely shredded
                4 carrots, sliced
                6 fresh green beans, cut
                1 medium can (6 oz.) snappy tomato juice
                Salt, pepper and garlic salt to taste

Brown beef and pour off grease. Add remaining ingredients and
cook for 1 1/2 to 2 hours. Remove from heat, cover and chill in
refrigerator overnight for seasonings to mix well.

Delicious the next day when re-warmed.

CREAM OF CORN SOUP
                                                             Serves 4

                1 (17 oz.) can cream style corn
                3/4 quart of regular milk
                1 onion, chopped
                Pat of butter
                Salt and pepper to taste

Blend above ingredients in blender. In a double boiler heat
mixture over low to medium heat for 1 1/2 to 2 hours. Chill in
refrigerator overnight. This is better made a day ahead and
warmed just before serving.

EASY FISH CHOWDER

  1 can cream of tomato soup
  1 can cream of mushroom soup
  1 jar cream of spinach babyfood
  1 can minced clams
  1 can crab
  1 pint Half and Half
  1 Cup sherry

Mix ingredients together. Store in covered container overnight.

WHEN READY TO SERVE - Heat slowly until hot.

GAZPACHO

  1 clove garlic, minced
  6 large ripe tomatoes, peeled, seeded and finely chopped
  2 cucumbers, peeled, seeded and finely chopped
  1/2 Cup sweet red pepper, minced
  1/2 Cup green pepper, minced
  1/2 Cup onion, minced
  2 Cups fresh tomato juice
  1/3 Cup olive oil
  3 Tbsp. lemon juice
  Salt, pepper and Tabasco to taste
  Sour cream (garnish)

Mix ingredients together, cover and chill overnight in refrigerator.

WHEN READY TO SERVE - Serve in chilled bowls and sprinkle with chopped parsley and a dollop of sour cream.

ITALIAN PEASANT SOUP

             1 1/2 lbs. ground beef
             1 onion, chopped
             1 1/2 lbs. fresh green beans, remove strings
             2 cans beef bouillon
             4 carrots, sliced
             1 large can tomatoes
             2 small cans tomato sauce
             2 cans garbanzo beans
             12 oz. macaroni or small shells, cooked
             Dash of sweet basil, oregano, salt, pepper, onion
             and garlic salt.
             Romano and Parmesan cheese (garnish)

In a large soup pot, saute meat with onion. Add liquid from cans,
tomatoes, green beans and carrots. Cook until green beans are
tender. Add garbanzo beans and macaroni and stir.

Can be made a day ahead and refrigerated overnight.

WHEN READY TO SERVE - Heat well and top soup with grated cheeses.

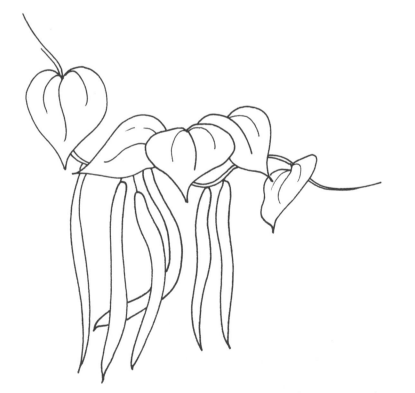

QUICK MINESTRONE SOUP   Serves 4

          3/4 lb. ground beef
          1 onion, chopped
          1 1/2 tsp. margarine
          1 can tomato soup
          1 can beef vegetable soup
          1 can beef bouillon
          2 ozs. fine noodles
          1 can kidney beans
          Parmesan cheese, grated (garnish)

Saute beef with onion in margarine. Add soups and noodles and
simmer for 20 minutes. Add kidney beans with liquid. Store in
covered container in refrigerator overnight so flavors blend.

WHEN READY TO SERVE - Serve warm topped with Parmesan cheese.

SPLIT PEA SOUP

          1 Cup split peas
          2 peeled potatoes
          1 onion
          1 carrot, peeled
          1 ham hock or bone
          3 quarts water
          2 Tbsp. ketchup

In a large soup kettle add water and place potatoes, onion, carrot
and ham hock. Boil for one hour. Remove ham bone and strain
ingredients through a sieve. Add split peas and boil for another
hour. Remove from heat, season with ketchup. Chill in
refrigerator covered overnight. Heat well before serving.

VEGETABLE BEEF SOUP   Serves 6-8

        1 to 2 lbs. beef, cut in small pieces
        1 (16 oz.) can tomatoes
        2 carrots, sliced
        3 celery stalks with tops, diced
        2 medium onions, diced
        2 medium potatoes, diced
        3 cups water
        1 tsp. salt
        4 peppercorns
        3 beef bouillon cubes
        1 pkg. (10 oz.) frozen mixed vegetables

Place all ingredients in a crock-pot. Cover and cook for 12 to 24
hours. Delicious.

TOMATO BISQUE   Serves 10-12

        1/4 lb. butter
        1 Cup celery, chopped
        1 Cup onion, chopped
        1/3 Cup flour
        7 Cups canned chopped tomatoes
        2 tsp. sugar
        1 tsp. basil
        1 tsp. marjoram
        1 Bay leaf
        4 Cups chicken broth
        1 pint whipping cream
        1/2 tsp. paprika
        1/2 tsp. curry powder
        Salt and pepper to taste

Saute celery, onion and carrots in butter until tender. Stir in
flour and cook for 2 minutes, stirring constantly. Add tomatoes,
sugar, spices and chicken broth. Cover and simmer 30 minutes,
stirring occasionally. Discard Bay leaf. Puree mixture, 1/2 at a
time in food processor. Add cream, paprika, curry powder, salt
and pepper. Stir to blend. Store in covered container in
refrigerator. It will keep several days or it can be frozen.

WHEN READY TO SERVE - Can be served hot or cold.

CREAM OF ZUCCHINI SOUP

                                                                Serves 8

                    3 Tbsp. margarine
                    3 Tbsp. onion, finely chopped
                    2 Cups chicken broth
                    1/2 tsp. salt
                    1/4 tsp. pepper
                    Dash of curry
                    1 Cup Half and Half
                    6 small or 3 large zucchini, sliced

In a large saucepan, saute onions in margarine. Add half of the
chicken broth and seasonings. Bring to a boil. Add zucchini,
cover and reduce heat. Simmer until tender. Remove from heat,
add rest of broth and slowly add half and half. Process mixture
in blender. Chill covered overnight in refrigerator.

WHEN READY TO SERVE - Can be served hot or cold.

AVOCADO VICHYSSOISE

                                                                Serves 6

                    2 ripe avocados
                    1 Cup Mocha Mix
                    1 tsp. lemon juice
                    Dash of onion juice or onion powder
                    5 Cups chicken broth, strained
                    Salt and pepper to taste
                    Chives (garnish)
                    Sour cream (garnish)

Puree avocado in processor. Slowly add chicken broth, Mocha Mix
and remaining ingredients. Blend until smooth. Chill in covered
container and serve cold.

WHEN READY TO SERVE - Serve cold and garnish with chives and a
dollop of sour cream.

Vegetables

ARTICHOKE PIE

Serves 6-8

    2 (9 oz.) pkgs. frozen artichoke hearts, cooked
    4 Tbsp. butter
    1/2 Cup onion, chopped
    1 Tbsp. flour
    1/2 Cup half and half
    1/2 Cup sour cream
    4 eggs, beaten
    Salt, pepper and nutmeg to taste
    2 tsp. parsley, minced
    1/2 Cup cheddar cheese, grated
    1/2 Cup Swiss cheese, grated
    1/4 Cup Parmesan cheese, grated
    1 prepared pie shell

Make a sauce of butter, onion, flour and half and half. Add sour cream, eggs and seasonings. Place artichoke hearts into a pie shell and sprinkle with Swiss and cheddar cheeses. Add sauce and top with Parmesan cheese.

Bake for 45 minutes at 350°.

When cool, cover with foil and refrigerate overnight. To serve, warm in slow oven.

ASPARAGUS AND PEA CASSEROLE

Serves 8

        2 (10 oz.) pkgs. frozen asparagus
        1 (10 oz.) pkg. frozen petite peas
        1 (6 oz.) jar sliced mushrooms, drained
        1 (2 oz.) jar diced pimento, drained
        3 Tbsp. butter or margarine
        3 Tbsp. flour
        3/4 Cup milk
        1 (5 oz.) jar sharp processed cheese spread
        1/4 tsp. salt
        1/8 tsp. pepper
        1/2 Cup fine dry bread crumbs
        3 Tbsp. butter or margarine

Cook asparagus and peas separately according to package directions. Drain (reserve liquid) and set aside. Cut asparagus into 2" pieces. In a buttered casserole, layer asparagus, peas, mushrooms and pimento. Set aside.

Over low heat, melt butter. Add flour, stirring until smooth. Cook for 1 minute. Combine reserved liquid from asparagus and pea waters making 3/4 cups and add to milk. Add to butter mixture and stir until smooth and slightly thickened. Stir in cheese spread, salt and pepper. Pour over vegetables.

Combine bread crumbs with melted butter and sprinkle over casserole. Cover and refrigerate overnight.

WHEN READY TO SERVE - Let stand for 30 minutes at room temperature. Bake uncovered for 40 minutes or until thoroughly heated.

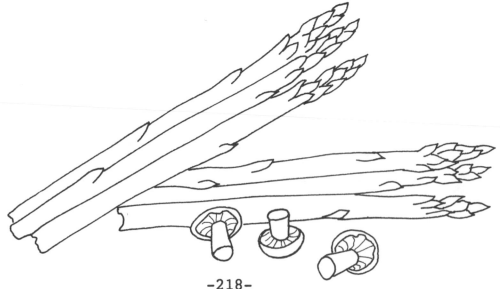

BAKED BEANS

Serves 12

        1 large (#2) can pork and beans
        3 tall cans baked beans
        1 Bell pepper, chopped
        2 onions, chopped
        1/3 Cup molasses
        1/3 Cup Worcestershire sauce
        1/2 lb. bacon, chopped
        1 cup brown sugar

Mix all ingredients together and bake in a casserole for 1 1/2
hours in a 325° oven.

Make a day ahead for a better flavor.

HOMEMADE BAKED BEANS

Serves 12

        2 lbs. dried Great Northern beans
        1 lb. bacon, cut into pieces
        2 Cups sugar
        1 large onion, quartered
        Salt to taste

Cover beans with water in a large sauce pan. Soak overnight.
The next day, pour off water and again, cover with cold water.
Add onion and boil until bean skins curl when you blow on them.

In a buttered casserole, layer beans, sugar and bacon. Ending
with sugar. Cover and refrigerate overnight.

Six to seven hours before serving time place casserole uncovered
into a 325° oven. Bake until ready to serve.

Easy to make and delicious!

SWEET AND SOUR BAKED BEANS

Serves 10

        8 slices bacon
        4 onions, sliced
        1/2 Cup brown sugar
        1 tsp. dry mustard
        1/2 tsp. garlic powder
        1 tsp. salt
        1/2 Cup cider vinegar
        2 (15 oz.) cans butter beans
        1 (16 oz.) can green lima beans
        1 (16 oz.) can kidney beans

Fry bacon until crisp. Remove bacon from pan and crumble. Set
aside. In bacon fat, add separated onion rings and cook until
clear, not browned. Add sugar, mustard, garlic powder, salt and
vinegar. Cover and simmer for 15 minutes. Remove from heat and
add beans and bacon. Pour into a 3-quart casserole, cover and
refrigerate overnight.

WHEN READY TO SERVE - Bake for 1 hour at 350°.

GREEN BEAN CASSEROLE

Serves 8

    2 pkgs. (10 oz.) frozen French cut green beans,
       thawed and dry
    1 onion, chopped
    1 can bean sprouts, drained
    1 can water chestnuts, drained and sliced
    1 can cream of mushroom soup
    1 Mozzarella ball, grated
    1 can French fried onion rings

Saute green beans and onion. Excluding onion rings, add remaining
ingredients and mix well. Top with onion rings. Pour into a
buttered casserole, cover and refrigerate overnight.

WHEN READY TO SERVE - Bake for 30 minutes at 350° or until
browned.

SWISS GREEN BEANS

Serves 6-8

    2 pkgs. (10 oz.) frozen French style green beans, cooked
    3 Tbsp. flour
    2 Tbsp. butter
    2 Cups sour cream
    1 medium onion, finely chopped
    1/4 tsp. salt
    1 (8 oz.) pkg. Swiss cheese, grated
    1/2 Cup slivered almonds (garnish)

Place beans in buttered casserole. Blend flour, butter and
gradually add sour cream, stirring constantly over low heat. Add
onion and salt. Cook until thickened, stirring constantly. Add
cheese and stir until melted. Pour over beans. Cover and
refrigerate overnight.

WHEN READY TO SERVE - Bake for 20 minutes at 350°. Top with
almonds and serve.

LIMA BEAN CASSEROLE

Serves 6-8

        1 lb. large dried lima beans
        6 Cups water
        8 whole cloves
        1 large onion, peeled and quartered
        1/2 Cup maple syrup
        1/2 Cup ketchup
        1 tsp. salt
        2 tsp. Worcestershire sauce
        1/4 tsp. pepper
        1 bay leaf
        1/4 lb. salt pork, cut into pieces

Rinse beans. Place in a 3-quart saucepan. Add water, cloves and onion. Boil for 5 minutes. Pour into a 3-quart casserole, cover and let stand overnight.

THE NEXT DAY - Add remaining ingredients. Bake covered in 300° oven for 2 1/2 hours. Uncover and bake for an additional 30 minutes stirring occasionally.

BROCCOLI CASSEROLE
                                                        Serves 6

       2 (10 oz.) pkgs. frozen chopped broccoli, cooked and drained
       2 eggs, beaten
       1 Cup mayonnaise
       1 can cream of mushroom soup
       1 Cup sharp Cheddar cheese, grated
       Potato chips

Excluding potato chips mix ingredients together. In a buttered
casserole (13" x 9") pour in mixture. Cover and refrigerate
overnight.

WHEN READY TO SERVE - Bake for 25 minutes in 350° oven. Remove
from oven, top with crushed potato chips and return to oven for
10 minutes to brown the top.

BROCCOLI AND RICE
                                                        Serves 6-8

       2 Cups rice, cooked
       1 (10 oz.) frozen pkg. chopped broccoli
       1 Cup water chestnuts, sliced
       1 (8 oz.) jar Cheese Whiz
       1 can cream of chicken soup
       1/2 Cup milk
       3 Tbsp. butter
       1/2 Cup celery, chopped
       1/4 onion, chopped

Blanch broccoli, drain and set aside. In a large bowl mix
together the remaining ingredients. Add broccoli and pour into a
buttered casserole. Cover and refrigerate overnight to bring out
the flavors.

WHEN READY TO SERVE - Bake for 45 minutes in a 325° oven or until
bubbly and browned.

STUFFED CARROTS

Serves 6

    12 medium carrots, scraped
    1/2 Cup rice, cooked
    1/2 Cup dry bread crumbs
    1/3 Cup Cheddar cheese, grated
    1/2 tsp. salt
    1/8 tsp. pepper
    1 tsp. onion, finely chopped
    1 tsp. green onion, finely chopped
    2 Tbsp. butter or margarine
    Parsley, chopped (garnish)
    Carrot curls (optional garnish)
    Parsley sprigs (optional garnish)

Cut whole carrots into 3" pieces. Cook carrots in a small amount
of water for 20 minutes or until tender, but firm. Let cool.
Core out center of each carrot.

Excluding garnish options, combine rice with remaining
ingredients. Stuff each carrot with mixture and place in a
buttered 13" x 9" x 2" baking dish. Cover and chill overnight.

WHEN READY TO SERVE - Remove from refrigerator and let stand at
room temperature for 30 minutes. Bake uncovered for 15 minutes in
350° oven. Garnish and serve hot.

CARROT CASSEROLE

Serves 6

    6 carrots, sliced
    3/4 Cup mayonnaise
    Juice from 1 lemon
    1 heaping Tbsp. horseradish
    Cheddar cheese, grated

Blanch carrots and rinse until cold. Place carrots in a buttered
casserole. Excluding cheese, mix together remaining ingredients
and spoon over top of carrots. Top with cheese. Cover and
refrigerate overnight.

WHEN READY TO SERVE - Bake for 15 to 20 minutes in a 350° oven.

CAULIFLOWER CREOLE

Serves 8

        3 Cups cauliflower, cooked and cut into small pieces
        2 Tbsp. butter
        1 onion, grated
        1/2 green pepper, chopped
        3 Tbsp. flour
        2 Cups fresh tomatoes, diced
        3 slices of bacon, cooked and crumbled (garnish)
        1/2 Cup cheese, grated (garnish)

Saute onion and green pepper. Add flour and tomatoes. Cook for 3
minutes. In a buttered casserole layer half of the cauliflower,
and half of sauce. Repeat layers. Cover and refrigerate
overnight.

WHEN READY TO SERVE - Bake for 20-25 minutes in a 350° oven.
Brown under broiler with cheese and bacon topping.

Wonderful side dish to serve with meat and a salad.

CREAMY CELERY BAKE

Serves 8

```
4 Cups celery, sliced thin
4 Tbsp. butter or margarine
3 Tbsp. flour
1 tsp. salt
1 Cup milk
1 (3 oz.) can chopped mushrooms, drained
2 Tbsp. green pepper, chopped
2 Tbsp. pimento, chopped
4 oz. sharp American cheese, grated
1 Cup soft bread crumbs
2 Tbsp. butter or margarine, melted
```

Saute celery in butter until tender. About 5 minutes. Set aside. In the same skillet add flour and salt. Add milk and cook until mixture is smooth and thickened. Add mushrooms, green pepper and pimentos. Add cheese and stir until melted. In a (10" x 6" x 1 1/2") baking dish place celery on bottom. Pour cheese mixture over the top. Top with bread crumbs and melted butter. Cover and refrigerate overnight.

WHEN READY TO SERVE - Bake for 20 minutes in a 350° oven.

STUFFED CELERY

Makes 30

```
10 stalks celery, cut into 3" pieces
 1 (8 oz.) pkg. cream cheese, softened
1/4 Cup mayonnaise
 1 Cup pecans, chopped
 1 clove garlic, crushed
 1 tsp. Beau Monde seasoning
1/4 Cup parsley, minced
Paprika (garnish)
```

Excluding celery and paprika, mix together remaining ingredients. Spoon into celery pieces and sprinkle with paprika. Cover and chill overnight.

CORN AU GRATIN

Serves 8

    3 eggs, beaten
    1 Cup half and half
    2 (17 oz.) cans cream-style corn
    1 pat of butter, melted
    Salt and pepper to taste
    1 Tbsp. sugar
    1 Cup Cheddar cheese, grated

Beat eggs with half and half. Add corn, sugar, salt, pepper and butter. In a buttered casserole pour mixture. Cover and refrigerate overnight.

WHEN READY TO SERVE - Sprinkle cheese on top and bake for 45 minutes in a 350° oven.

This is so good that everyone will want your recipe.

PEAS ORIENTAL

Serves 12

    3 (10 oz.) pkgs. frozen peas, cooked
    2 (16 oz.) cans water chestnuts, drained and sliced thinly
    2 (20 oz.) cans bean sprouts, drained
    1 lb. fresh mushrooms, sliced
    2 (10 1/2 oz.) cans cream of mushroom soup
    2 (3 1/2 oz.) cans French fried onion rings

Saute mushrooms and peas together quickly. Drain and set aside. Add soup, and excluding onion rings, add remaining ingredients. Mix well and pour into buttered casserole. Cover and refrigerate overnight.

WHEN READY TO SERVE - Bake for 30 minutes at 350°. Remove from oven and top with onions rings. Cook for an additional 15 minutes or until lightly browned on top. Serve hot.

POTATO CASSEROLE

Serves 8-10

    6 medium potatoes, boiled with skins on
    2 Tbsp. butter
    3 Cups corn flakes, crushed
    1 can cream of mushroom soup
    1/4 Cup butter
    1 pint sour cream
    1 Cup Cheddar cheese, grated
    1/2 Cup green onion, chopped fine

Grate potatoes with skins on. Set aside. Mix 2 Tbsp. butter with
corn flakes. Set aside. Heat together soup and 1/4 Cup butter.
Set aside. Mix together sour cream, cheese and onion. Set aside.
In a buttered casserole layer potatoes, soup mixture and cheese
sauce. Top with corn flake topping.   To allow seasoning this
recipe is best made a day ahead.

WHEN READY TO SERVE - Bake for 45 minutes in a 350° oven.

BAKED POTATO SALAD

Serves 8

    6 medium potatoes, cooked and sliced
    3 Tbsp. fine bread crumbs
    6 hard-cooked eggs, chopped
    1/4 Cup butter, melted
    2 Tbsp. flour
    1 1/2 Cups sour cream
    1 1/2 Cups mayonnaise
    1 1/2 Tbsp. chives, chopped

Sprinkle a buttered 2-quart casserole with 1 Tbsp. of bread
crumbs. Combine sour cream, mayonnaise, flour and chives. Place
a layer of potatoes, salted to taste, one half of the eggs and dot
with cream mixture. Repeat the layers. Cover with remaining
cream mixture. Sprinkle top with bread crumbs and dot with
butter. Cover and chill in refrigerator overnight.

WHEN READY TO SERVE - Bake uncovered for 25-30 minutes in a 350°
oven or until thoroughly warmed through and top is browned.

POTATO SOUFFLE

Serves 6

    2 Cups mashed potatoes
    1 (8 oz.) pkg. cream cheese
    8 oz. sour cream
    2 eggs
    1/2 Cup Milk
    1 small onion, diced
    2 Tbsp. flour
    Salt and pepper to taste
    1 (3 1/2 oz.) can French fried onions

Mash potatoes in a large bowl. Mix in milk. Add softened cheese, sour cream, eggs, onion and flour. Beat at low speed until blended, then at high speed until fluffy and light. Add salt and pepper to taste. In a buttered round 9" baking dish place potato mixture. Cover and refrigerate overnight.

WHEN READY TO SERVE - Sprinkle with fried onions and bake in moderate oven for 35-40 minutes until hot and browned on top.

STUFFED BAKED POTATOES

Serves 6

    6 large potatoes, baked
    1 Cup sour cream
    1/2 cube butter
    2 green onions, chopped
    1 Cup Cheddar cheese, grated
    Salt, pepper and garlic salt to taste

Cut off tops of baked potatoes, scooping out potato into a large mixing bowl. Mash potato with the above ingredients. Reserve half of cheese before refilling potato skins. Top with remaining cheese. Cover and refrigerate until ready to serve.

WHEN READY TO SERVE - Bake uncovered in moderate oven for 30-45 minutes or until warmed and brown on top.

This recipe is easy and always a favorite.

ONIONS IN ONIONS

Serves 4

        4 large Bermuda onions
        1 cube butter
        1/2 to 3/4 Cups milk
       12 pearl onions
        2 Tbsp. flour
        Salt and pepper to taste
        Buttered bread crumbs

Using a wire whisk melt butter while stirring in flour until
mixture is crumbly. Reduce heat and slowly stir in milk.
Increase heat and stir until thick. Remove from heat and set
aside. Parboil all onions in order to remove skins. Scoop out
insides of Bermuda onions. Add pearl onions to white sauce.
Stuff each Bermuda onion with pearl onion mixture and top with
bread crumbs. Cover and refrigerate overnight.

WHEN READY TO SERVE - Heat onions in a medium oven for 15 minutes
and put under broiler to brown tops.

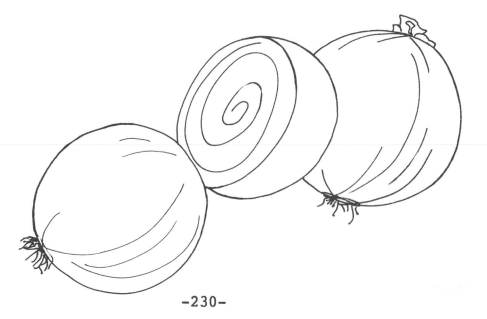

BOURBON SWEET POTATOES

Serves 6-8

      2 (29 oz.) cans sweet potatoes, drained and mashed
      3/4 Cup brown sugar, firmly packed
      1/2 Cup butter or margarine, melted
      1/4 - 1/2 Cup bourbon
      1/2 tsp. vanilla
      2 Cups miniature marshmallows

Excluding marshmallows, combine ingredients. Mix well. Spoon
mixture into a lightly oiled 1 1/2-quart casserole. Cover and
refrigerate overnight.

WHEN READY TO SERVE - Allow to stand for 30 minutes at room
temperature before baking for 25 minutes at 350°. Remove from
oven, top with marshmallows and bake an additional 7 minutes or
until golden brown.

SWEET POTATO CASSEROLE

Serves 8-10

      6-8 sweet potatoes or yams
      1/2 Cup butter
      1 Cup brown sugar
      2 egg yolks, beaten
      1/2 Cup sherry
      1 tsp. nutmeg
      2 egg whites, beaten stiff

Boil potatoes in jackets, peel and put through a ricer, or mash.
Cream butter, sugar and egg yolks together. Add sherry and
nutmeg. Mix mixture well with mashed potatoes. Fold in stiffly
beaten egg whites. Fold into a buttered casserole, cover and
chill in refrigerator overnight.

WHEN READY TO SERVE - Bake in 350° oven for 30 minutes or until
brown on top and warmed thoroughly.

BERRY MALLOW YAM BAKE

Serves 6-8

    1/2 Cup flour
    1/2 Cup brown sugar
    1/2 Cup old fashioned or
        quick oats, uncooked
    1 tsp. cinnamon
    1/3 Cup margarine, cold
    2 cans (17 oz.) yams, drained and sliced
    2 Cups fresh cranberries, raw
    1 1/2 Cups miniature marshmallows

Cut margarine into flour, sugar, oats and cinnamon until it
resembles coarse crumbs. With 1 cup of coarse crumbs add yams and
cranberries. Place in a buttered 1 1/2 quart casserole. Top with
remaining coarse crumbs. Cover and refrigerate overnight.

WHEN READY TO SERVE - Top casserole with 1 1/2 Cups miniature
marshmallows. Bake at 350° until brown on top and bubbly hot.

SPANAKOITIPUPETES (GREEK CASSEROLE)

Serves 6

         2 eggs
         1 medium onion, quartered
         1/2 lb. Feta cheese, grated
         1 (3 oz.) pkg. cream cheese
         1 (10 oz.) pkg. frozen chopped spinach, thawed and dry
         2 Tbsp. parsley, chopped
         1 Tbsp. fresh dill, chopped
           or 1 tsp. dill seed
         Dash of pepper
         2 pkgs. fillo (prepared dough at deli)
         1 Cup butter or margarine, melted

Add to dry spinach, egg and onion. Mix well. Combine cheeses and
herbs. Mix until just combined. Cover and refrigerate
overnight.

WHEN READY TO SERVE - Spread out fillo dough and brush each piece
with melted butter. Cover the bottom of a buttered casserole with
six layers of buttered fillo dough. Top with a layer of spinach
mixture. Repeat with six layers of fillo dough and spinach
mixture. Repeat to top, ending with fillo dough. Brush top layer
of dough with butter and bake for 20 minutes in a 375° oven.

ZUCCHINI CASSEROLE

Serves 6

     2 lbs. zucchini, sliced
     1/4 Cup onion, chopped
     1 can cream of chicken soup
     1 Cup sour cream
     1 Cup carrots, grated
     1 (8 oz.) pkg. seasoned stuffing mix
     1/2 Cup butter
     Salt to taste

In boiling water cook zucchini and onion together for 3 minutes.
Drain and mix vegetables with carrots. Combine soup and sour
cream and mix with vegetables. Add salt to taste. Combine butter
to stuffing mix. In a buttered (12" x 7" x 2") casserole spread
1/2 of the stuffing mix on bottom and vegetables on top. Top with
remaining stuffing mix. Cover and refrigerate overnight.

WHEN READY TO SERVE - Bake at 350° for 25-30 minutes.

ZUCCHINI CHEESE CASSEROLE

Serves 8-10

     4-5 large zucchini, grated
     1/2 lb. Cheddar cheese, grated
     1 onion, grated
     1 stack of Ritz crackers, crushed
     6 eggs, beaten
     Salt and pepper to taste
     Parmesan cheese, grated

Mix together crackers, eggs, salt and pepper. Add cheese and
vegetable and mix well. Pour into a buttered casserole. Top with
Parmesan cheese. Cover and refrigerate overnight.

WHEN READY TO SERVE - Bake for 3/4 to 1 hour at 350° or until
browned and egg has set.

WILD RICE CASSEROLE

Serves 6-8

        2/3 Cups wild rice, washed
        1 lb. ground round
        1 onion, chopped
        1 can cream of mushroom soup
        1 can cream of chicken soup
        1/2 Cup water
        1/8 tsp. garlic salt
        1/8 tsp. celery salt
        1/8 tsp. salt
        1/8 tsp. pepper
        1/2 lb. small fresh mushrooms or
            1 can of mushrooms, drained
        Parmesan cheese (garnish)

Saute ground round and onions together until meat is crumbly.
Drain off fat and add remaining ingredients. Mix well. Pour into
a buttered casserole. Top with Parmesan cheese. Cover and
refrigerate overnight.

WHEN READY TO SERVE - Bake uncovered for 1 hour in a 350° oven.

STUFFED ZUCCHINI

Serves 6

    6 small/medium zucchini
    2 Cups soft bread crumbs
    2 Tbsp. butter, melted
    1/2 Cup salami, finely chopped
    1 egg, slightly beaten
    1 Tbsp. water
    1/4 onion, chopped
    1 Tbsp. parsley, chopped
    1/2 Tbsp. poultry seasoning
    1/4 tsp. salt
    1/8 tsp. pepper
    Parmesan cheese (garnish)

Cut zucchini in half, lengthwise. Scoop out seeded area. Blanch
zucchini, drain and set aside. Excluding cheese, mix together the
above ingredients. Fill each zucchini with breaded mixture. Dot
with butter and sprinkle cheese on top and place in greased
casserole. Cover and refrigerate overnight.

WHEN READY TO SERVE - Bake for 25-30 minutes in 375° oven.

This is a delicious side dish to serve with meat and salad.

BREADS:

BREAKFAST AND BRUNCH:

DESSERTS:

DESSERTS: (cont.)

ENTREES: (cont.)

HOLIDAY TREATS:

SALADS: (cont.)

IF YOU FIND ANY ERRORS IN OUR RECIPES,

PLEASE TAKE INTO CONSIDERATION THAT

"MAMA JUST ISN'T WHAT SHE USED TO BE!"